BLOOM'S ReViews

COMPREHENSIVE RESEARCH & STUDY GUIDES

Arthur Miller's

The Crucible

Edited & with
an Introduction
by Harold Bloom

First Printing
1 3 5 7 9 8 6 4 2

ISBN: 0-7910-4117-4

Chelsea House Publishers
1974 Sproul Road, Suite 400
P.O. Box 914
Broomall, PA 19008-0914

The Chelsea House World Wide Web addre
http://www.chelseahouse.com

Contents

Editor's Note

My Introduction compares *The Crucible* to Shaw's *Saint Joan* and suggests that Miller's play, unlike Shaw's, someday will seem a period piece. Robert Warshaw confirms that suggestion by linking the play to American politics of the 1950s, while David Levin finds Miller's invocation of the Salem witch trials to be wholly appropriate. Absolute evil is ascribed by Miller himself to the prosecutors, both in Puritan Salem and in contemporary America.

Both Paul West and Sheila Huftel try to expand *The Crucible*'s scope by emphasizing its tragic dignity rather than its politics. Stage revision is examined by Jean Gould, and Miller's style by Stephen Fender, while Edward Murray emphasizes issues of emotional complexity in the characters.

Miller's political difficulties, as caused by *The Crucible*, are cited by Leonard Moss, after which Benjamin Nelson praises Miller as an analyst of group hysteria. Chadwick Hansen angrily accuses Miller of racism in his portrait of Tituba, while Orm Överland condemns Miller for spoiling the drama with tiresome revisions.

C. W. E. Bigsby criticizes Miller for depicting the play's authority figures only in external terms, after which E. Miller Budick examines how Miller handles history for his purposes. The eminent historian Edmund S. Morgan judges Miller's understanding of Puritanism to be inadequate, while Dennis Welland approves of Miller's use of his sources. Hale's transformation from persecutor to doubter is traced by Robert A. Martin, after which Iska Alter examines the varied roles of women in *The Crucible*.

The ironies of societal anxiety are analyzed by Richard G. Sacharine as being central to the play, and in the final critical extract, James J. Martine expounds Miller's metaphor of the crucible, the hard trial or test that Proctor must undergo.

Introduction

HAROLD BLOOM

In his introduction to his *Collected Plays* (1957), Arthur Miller returned to *The Crucible,* produced four years before, but he went back with an anguish provoked by the after-effects of McCarthyism, the witch-hunt of the 1950s, led by Senator Joe McCarthy and his lawyer-disciple, Roy Cohn. In 1954, Miller had been refused a passport by our State Department, so that he was unable to attend the opening of *The Crucible* in Brussels. Miller's authentic ordeal came in 1956, when he appeared before the House Un-American Activities Committee and declined to name suspected communists, which led to a conviction of contempt of Congress in 1957. Though his conviction was reversed by the Supreme Court a year later, Miller's crisis is vividly conveyed in the 1957 introduction to his *Collected Plays:*

> It was not only the rise of "McCarthyism" that moved me, but something which seemed much more weird and mysterious. It was the fact that a political, objective, knowledgeable campaign from the far Right was capable of creating not only a terror, but a new subjective reality, a veritable mystique which was gradually assuming even a holy resonance. The wonder of it all struck me that so practical and picayune a cause, carried forward by such manifestly ridiculous men, should be capable of paralyzing thought itself, and worse, causing to billow up such persuasive clouds of "mysterious" feelings within people. It was as though the whole country had been born anew, without a memory even of certain elemental decencies which a year or two earlier no one would have imagined could be altered, let alone forgotten. Astounded, I watched men pass me by without a nod whom I had known rather well for years; and again, the astonishment was produced by my knowledge, which I could not give up, that the terror in these people was being knowingly planned and consciously engineered, and yet that all they knew was terror. That so interior and subjective an emotion could have been so manifestly created from without was a marvel to. me. It underlies every word in *The Crucible.*

It is not quite forty years since Miller composed these tense sentences, but one wonders whether they may not prove prophetic as we approach Millennium. Anti-communism is a faded banner since the demise of the Soviet Union, but witch-hunting takes many forms in the United States, and can be heard daily in the rhetoric of the Christian Coalition, the National Rifle Association, our rabid militia movements, and indeed the Gingrichian Republican party. Un-Americans are variously identified as homosexuals, Satanists, residents of New York City, or whatever, and once again an emotion "so interior and subjective" is being "created from without." *The Crucible*, alas, is likely to go on being as relevant a drama as it was back in 1953, when first it was staged.

Eric Bentley, still the most intelligent and best informed of our dramatic critics, has pointed to the ways in which the genres of tragedy and of social drama tend to destroy one another in Miller's work. *The Crucible*, according to Bentley, rather too neatly separated the liberal sheep and the persecut-ing goats. Still worse, Bentley remarked that "one never knows what a Miller play is about: politics or sex." Is *The Crucible* a drama of adultery or of moral conscience confronting a perse-cuting society? How convincing is Miller's presentation of his-torical Salem and its obsessed self-destructiveness? *The Crucible* is certainly a successful stage play; revival follows revival, both here and in Great Britain. As a well-made play, *The Crucible* might seem to challenge comparison with George Bernard Shaw's *Saint Joan*, yet clearly it is not of *Saint Joan's* eminence, and in fact may owe a good deal to Shaw's drama that culminates in a public burning. Miller is Ibsen's disciple (as Shaw was), and not Shaw's, and yet *The Crucible* is a curiously Shavian play, as Dennis Welland has demonstrated. Welland shrewdly pointed to the repetition of "I think" by several of the drama's characters and found in this verbal formula "a very skillfully-managed way of suggesting the scruples, the misgiv-ings, and the conscientious earnestness which are all that these people can bring against the diabolic impetus of the witch-hunt." One can agree with Welland in relating this concern with conscience, and with our incapacity to understand authen-tic evil, to Shaw's *Saint Joan*, while worrying (as Welland does not) whether Shaw simply overwhelms Miller. So many elements in Miller's design are so close to Shaw's as to tran-scend the possibility of accident, and yet Shaw's power of morally ironic comedy is totally alien to Miller's sensibility and purposes.

Does *The Crucible* survive because it is a good theatre-piece whose relevance remains contemporary, or does it also possess, as *Saint Joan* does, a literary eminence entirely its own? A similar question is provoked by Tony Kushner's *Angels in America,* a two-play "epic fantasia on national themes" that meets our moment with grand immediacy, but that may, some day, become a period piece. An America cleansed of witch-hunting, in any mode, might find *The Crucible* another period piece, but that America, alas, is still to come. ❖

Biography of Arthur Miller

Arthur Miller was born on October 17, 1915, to Isadore and Augusta Barnett Miller, a well-to-do Jewish couple. The first fourteen years of his life were spent in upscale Harlem; then, when the stock market crash of 1929 and the subsequent depression nearly ruined his father, a manufacturer of ladies' coats, Miller's family moved to Brooklyn. He was an indifferent student, and upon graduating from Abraham Lincoln High School in 1932 he found that his grades were not good enough to get him into college—which, in any event, his family could not afford. Miller took a series of odd jobs, then worked for a year as a shipping clerk in an automobile parts warehouse. During this time he first began to read literature extensively. In 1934 Miller was accepted at the University of Michigan, where he enrolled as a journalism student and began to write plays.

His first two dramas, *No Villain* (1936) and *Honors at Dawn* (1937), both won minor awards, which encouraged him to pursue his ambitions as a playwright. By the time he graduated in 1938 he had completed one more play, as well as discovering the works of Henrik Ibsen; these became a lasting influence on his own writing. In 1939 he wrote a play, *The Golden Years,* for the Federal Theatre Project. This was followed by four or five other plays, none of which were produced at the time and all of which he found unsatisfactory. It was not until 1944 that he wrote *The Man Who Had All the Luck,* the first notable play of his mature period, and a qualified success in its author's eyes as well. It won the Theatre Guild National Award. This was followed by a nonfiction book, *Situation Normal* (1944), based on interviews with American servicemen, and then by *Focus* (1945), a novel about anti-Semitism.

Miller began to receive increasing critical notice with the production of his play *All My Sons* (1947), an Ibsenesque drama centered on the revelation of a small manufacturer's having supplied defective equipment under a government contract during the war. It was the next play that secured his reputation: *Death of a Salesman* (1949), the story of a failed traveling salesman and his family, became an instant classic of the American theatre and was awarded a Pulitzer Prize.

After publishing an adaptation of Henrik Ibsen's *An Enemy of the People* (1951), Miller wrote *The Crucible* (1953), which dealt with the Salem witch trials of 1692. This play was also well received, but it attracted critical attention of another sort. Miller's history of affiliation with leftist organizations brought him under the eye of Senator Joseph McCarthy and the House Un-American Activities Committee (HUAC) during their investigations of alleged communist infiltration of American institutions. Miller freely testified before the committee in his own behalf, but refused its requests that he name others who had been similarly involved. In the political climate of the time *The Crucible* was, perhaps understandably, read as a commentary on the McCarthyites' activities. Though HUAC found him an insufficiently friendly witness, Miller's career survived the experience, and his *A View from the Bridge,* presented in 1955 on a double bill with his short play *A Memory of Two Mondays,* brought him a second Pulitzer Prize.

In 1956 Miller divorced his wife of many years, Mary Grace Slattery Miller—whom he had married in 1940 and who had supported him and their two children during his unremunerative early writing career—and married the actress Marilyn Monroe. (His screenplay for the 1961 film *The Misfits,* directed by John Huston and starring Monroe and Clark Gable, was originally conceived as a vehicle for her.) After five years the second marriage ended in divorce, and in 1962 Miller married photographer Inge Morath, with whom he had two children; he also collaborated with her on several books, writing text to accompany her pictures.

In 1963 Miller published *Jane's Blanket,* a children's book. The next year his *After the Fall,* a semi-autobiographical, almost novelistic play whose action spans several decades, was produced to mixed notices; some critics panned it as self-indulgent, while others have praised its complex exploration of character and moral issues. It was followed by *Incident at Vichy* (1965), a short play about Nazism and anti-Semitism in Vichy France, and by *The Price* (1968) and *The American Clock* (produced 1980; published 1982), both of which return to Miller's earlier themes of domestic life and family conflicts. Other recent Miller plays include *The Archbishop's Ceiling* (produced 1977; published 1984), *The Last Yankee* (1991), *Broken Glass* (1994), and several short plays.

Besides his plays, Miller's other works include *I Don't Need You Anymore* (1967), a collection of short stories (an expanded edition was published in 1987 as *The Misfits and Other Stories*); *In Russia* (1969) and *In the Country* (1977), both with Inge Morath; and *The Theatre Essays of Arthur Miller* (1978), a volume of his previously uncollected short essays and criticism. Miller's trip to Beijing in 1983 to direct *Death of a Salesman* was written up in an autobiographical volume, *Salesman in Beijing* (1984), while *Timebends: A Life* (1987) is a more formal autobiography. Miller continues to live and write in Connecticut. ✤

Thematic and Structural Analysis

The philosopher George Santayana warned that those who cannot remember the past are condemned to repeat it. Arthur Miller wrote *The Crucible* to remind his contemporaries of a horrific episode in American history and to awaken his audience to the danger of its repetition. The chilling play is based on the Salem witch trials of 1692, which resulted in the hanging of nineteen persons and the death by torture of another. The tragic events that Miller re-creates were caused by the destructive power of mass fear and of guilt by implication. His admonishment is as timely today as it was in 1953.

In "A Note on the Historical Accuracy of This Play," the playwright explains that *The Crucible* does not follow history in any strictly academic sense. Certain circumstances of the trials are unknown to historians; for instance, the personalities of the individuals involved cannot be ascertained from surviving letters, records, and broadsides. Therefore, the author took the liberty to animate his characters. Miller also fused several historical persons into fewer characters: the number of girls who actually leveled accusations of witchcraft was greater according to the record than the number who appear as characters in the play. However, the author assures us that "there is no one in the drama who did not play a similar—and in some cases exactly the same—role in history."

In various intertextual notes, Miller draws clear parallels between the dualistic hyperbole of the Salem witch trials to accusations being made and events taking place during the composition of *The Crucible*—namely, the McCarthy hearings of the early 1950s. Increasingly, those called before the House Un-American Activities Committee (HUAC) were expected to clear themselves by accusing others of communist activity—in much the same way as those arrested in Salem were asked to do. When, in our own century, witnesses refused to implicate others, the proceedings were derailed—as Giles Corey, Rebecca Nurse, and John Proctor are able to thwart the court's momentum in *The Crucible*.

At one point Miller digresses from describing a main character, Reverend Hale, by discussing the demonizing of one's opponents, throughout history, as a political strategy. Miller writes:

> A political policy is equated with moral right, and opposition to it with diabolical malevolence. Once such an equation is effectively made, society becomes a congeries of plots and counterplots, and the main role of government changes from that of the arbiter to that of the scourge of God.

The author lists the face-off between communists and capitalists as one example. Two features of this phenomenon are consistent over time: the attempt to judge the intentions rather than the actions of a person and the condemnation of the sexual attitudes of one's opposition as being immoral.

The play's action is divided into four acts with no scene divisions. The second act was first written with two scenes; however, Miller deleted the second scene, and it is usually not performed (it appears in published copies of the play as an appendix). The uninterrupted pace of the action mimics how quickly the cry of witchcraft rose and how difficult it was to stop, given the level of hysterical projection. The settings appropriately move from the bedroom of Betty Parris in the first act to a jail cell in the last act, illustrating the extent to which private life and public punishment become merged together under the Puritans' theocratic system.

The play opens in **Act 1** in the bedroom of Betty Parris. Nearly all the major characters enter this small room, and much is revealed about their personalities. Reverend Parris is kneeling and praying beside his daughter's bed. He is torn between his desire to keep her illness private and his impulse to obtain the reassurance and assistance of others. Parris receives several visitors who are curious about Betty's strange symptoms. It is rumored that she has flown through the air, and many townspeople are gathered in Parris's foyer awaiting his explanation. We sense that some seek his reassurance while others look for an opportunity to attack him. In his interactions with each of his visitors, it is clear that Parris is more concerned with shielding his household from the charge of witchcraft than he is with nursing his daughter to health.

His first visitor is his slave Tituba, whom he drives from the room. Miller notes Tituba's sense that she will be held accountable for this calamity as she has been for previous troubles. From a conversation between Parris and his niece Abigail, we learn that the minister discovered his daughter Betty with Abigail and several other girls dancing in the forest with Tituba. Abigail swears to him that they were only dancing to Tituba's Barbados songs.

The Putnams enter. Their only daughter Ruth is afflicted with a similar trancelike condition. Mrs. Putnam considers the illnesses related to the infant deaths of seven of her children. The three go downstairs to quiet the crowd with a psalm and leave Abigail, Betty, and two other girls alone to discuss their predicament. We learn that Tituba led the girls in a conjuring ritual and that Ruth participated at her mother's request. Mrs. Putnam hoped her daughter could contact the souls of the departed infants. Abigail also drank a charm to kill Elizabeth Proctor, her former employer and the wife of John Proctor, with whom she had a sexual encounter. Betty awakens, and Abigail threatens revenge should Betty reveal the truth about the activities in the woods.

Betty returns to her inert state as John Proctor, looking for his servant Mary Warren, enters the room. He sends Mary home. Abigail tells Proctor that they were dancing in the woods and that Betty has merely taken fright at being discovered. She laughs off Proctor's remark that the town is calling it witchcraft. She blocks his exit and tells him that she waits for him nightly and that she knows he loves her. Proctor denies this and insists their sexual relationship never happened. Abigail insults Proctor's wife, and, after he rebukes her, she responds with what may be her only truthful speech:

> I look for John Proctor that took me from my sleep and put knowledge in my heart! I never knew what pretense Salem was, I never knew the lying lessons I was taught by all these Christian women and their covenanted men! And now you bid me tear the light out of my eyes? I will not, I cannot! You loved me, John Proctor, and whatever sin it is, you love me yet!

Parris and the Putnams return and are joined by Rebecca Nurse and Giles Corey. Both the Putnams and Parris look to

Rebecca for advice. Rebecca's surname is an appropriate description of her charitable role in the community. She is a figure of sensible restraint and reason. For example, when Mrs. Putnam views her daughter's lack of appetite as a sign of her being "bewildered," Rebecca calmly replies that Ruth may not be hungry. Other similarly absurd deductions made during the play would be humorous if they did not lead to such tragic ends. The author repeatedly illustrates how projected fear and hidden guilt prevent many of the characters from drawing the most simple and most logical conclusions.

Miller reveals the animosity between the men present in the room. Proctor distrusts both Reverend Parris and Thomas Putnam and indicates that he views Parris as having overstepped his authority in sending for Reverend Hale. Parris charges that many in the congregation are unmindful of their obligations and that he is underpaid. Putnam renews an argument over land and finds himself opposed by both Proctor and Giles Corey.

Reverend Hale, at Parris's request, arrives from the nearby town of Beverly. He is a learned man, eager to display his knowledge. He soothes everyone's nerves by his reassuring and complimentary nature. Under his intense questioning, Abigail admits that she drank blood in the woods, but that Tituba forced her to do so. Hale turns his interrogation toward Tituba. Parris threatens her with whipping, and Putnam calls for her hanging. Hale, however, assures her that if she confesses she will be protected. Relieved, Tituba admits to commerce with the Devil and, when prompted by Putnam, lists several local women as being enlisted by the Devil. Seeing how Tituba satisfied her inquisitors, Abigail confesses and lists more names of "witches." Betty wakes up and picks up the chant, providing additional names. The curtain falls as the girls continue to implicate more women.

Act 2 takes place in the common room of the Proctor home eight days after the action of Act 1. As John Proctor returns home late from seeding fields, his wife Elizabeth greets him suspiciously and questions him about his whereabouts. Fearing he has been in Salem with Abigail, Elizabeth strains to keep their interactions civil. They turn to discuss Mary Warren's

attendance at the trial, something Proctor has forbidden. Th
speak of the town having "gone wild," and Elizabeth encou
ages Proctor to inform the court of his conversation with
Abigail—her admission that Betty's affliction was not the result
of witchcraft. The couple argue about Proctor's hesitancy to do
so, and he is angered by Elizabeth's continued suspicions about
his unfaithfulness.

Mary Warren arrives and claims to be ill. She gives Elizabeth
a doll she sewed during the day, and she reports that thirty-
nine women have been arrested. Further, a beggar woman is
going to be hanged on Mary's testimony and on her failure to
recite the Ten Commandments. All three argue about Mary's
role in the trials. When Proctor threatens to whip her for her
disobedience, Mary claims she has saved Elizabeth from arrest.
She will not reveal who has implicated Elizabeth, however, and
she stomps off to bed.

Elizabeth convinces Proctor that Abigail intends to see her
arrested; they come to an understanding of their marriage's
tenuous condition despite the seven months' time since
Abigail's departure. As if to test their resolve, Hale arrives to
question the couple about the "monstrous attack upon the village" and about their own Christian character. The church
records show that Proctor has been absent from worship frequently, and one of the Proctor sons is not baptized. Proctor
explains that his disgust with Parris has driven him to worship
privately. When Hale asks Proctor to recite the Ten
Commandments, Elizabeth must supply "adultery" for him.
Proctor tries to disguise his pain at hearing the word from
Elizabeth's lips, and he tells Hale: "You see, between the two of
us we know them all." Of course, Hale does not see what has
transpired between them: a solidifying of their relationship
against a common foe—the trials. However, Proctor remains
overcome with guilt, and his final remark about forgetting the
sixth commandment is most ironic: "I think it be a small fault."
As Hale turns to leave, Elizabeth begs Proctor to reveal
Abigail's duplicity. He does so, but Hale chooses to have faith
in the confessions already extracted.

Giles Corey and Francis Nurse arrive to announce that their
wives have been arrested. Even Hale is troubled by this news.

Ezekiel Cheever enters with a warrant for Elizabeth's arrest: Abigail has charged Elizabeth with afflicting her with stomach pains by hexing her with a doll and a needle. Outraged, Proctor calls for Mary Warren, who admits she sewed the doll in court that day in Abigail's presence, but the doll is still taken as evidence against Elizabeth. Proctor shreds the warrant, but Elizabeth agrees to go with the marshalls. Hale suggests that only by their uncovering some greater evil can their wives be spared:

> The jails are packed—our greatest judges sit in Salem now—and hanging's promised. Man, we must look to cause proportionate. Were there murder done perhaps, and never brought to light? Abomination? Some secret blasphemy that stinks to heaven? Think on cause, man, and let you help me to discover it. For there's your way, believe it, there is your only way, when such confusion strikes upon the world.

Miller makes clear that one underlying "abomination" is John's illicit relationship with Abigail; as long as the affair remains secret, it is able to fuel a series of projections, false confessions, and cover-ups. Hale's remark is also prophetic: there are other hidden motives—prejudice, jealousy, and greed—that, if left uncovered, will continue to drive the accusations. Proctor, not yet able to accept that his confession is required, tries to convince Mary Warren to testify to the girls' fraud, but she cries emphatically that she cannot.

Act 2, Scene 2 (omitted by the author and usually not performed) shows a different side of Abigail, one that is not simply conniving and malevolent. Most of the motivational information supplied in this section, however, is already presented in other parts of the play. Proctor and Abigail meet in a wood at night. Proctor says that he hears that she is out nightly in the tavern with the deputy governor and is followed through town by a troop of boys. Abigail says such attention displeases her, that her spirit has changed entirely because of the godly work she does. She lifts her dress to show him the needle marks that she has suffered at the hands of the witches, including his wife. Proctor recognizes her insanity.

As in Act 1, she tells Proctor that it is he who has burned away her ignorance: "I will make you such a wife when the world is white again." Proctor tells her that he has come to warn her of his plans for tomorrow. His wife is thirty-six days in jail, and if Abigail will not free her, Proctor will expose Abigail as a fraud. If need be, he will also admit to their fornication. She does not believe him; she says he is happy that his wife will die, and she will save him from himself in the court the next day.

Act 3 opens in the empty vestry of the Salem meetinghouse, which has been converted into an anteroom for the court—the change in the room's purpose symbolizing the loss of the people's voice under theocratic law. Miller describes the walls as being constructed of boards "of random widths." The scenery represents what will be revealed during the act: the inconsistency of the legal structure before us.

Voices are heard from inside the courtroom. Judge Hathorne accuses Martha Corey of reading fortunes, which she denies. We never see Martha Corey, nor does she participate in the action of the play; yet hers is the only trial that is dramatized. The staging reminds us that she, like the rest of the accused, is convicted on the basis of unseen evidence. We hear Giles Corey, claiming that the court is hearing lies and that Thomas Putnam is manipulating the proceedings in order to gain land.

The marshall removes Corey to the vestry and into our view. Hathorne, Hale, Danforth, and Parris soon join him and question him about the evidence he claims to have for the court. Francis Nurse joins Corey in asserting that the girls are frauds. Danforth takes the charge not as new evidence, but as a personal attack against his credibility as a judge. He rebukes both men sharply.

Proctor enters with Mary Warren, and Hale, beginning to doubt the validity of the proceedings, encourages Danforth to hear her testimony. With Proctor amplifying her meek voice, she says that she saw no spirits and that the other girls are lying as well, that their afflictions in court were "pretense." Danforth is concerned that rumors of fraud in the village will lead to rebellion, and he questions Proctor's motives. Proctor insists that he has no desire to undermine the court and that he only wants to free his wife. Danforth tries to put him off by telling him that his wife Elizabeth claims to be pregnant, and if she is, her life will be spared for another year. At this point, morals and motives are indistinguishable to Danforth and his supporters.

Proctor, however, says he will maintain his charge of fraud on behalf of the wives of his friends, Corey and Nurse. Together the men present a document, signed by ninety-one people, testifying to their good opinion of the three accused women. Parris, as his name suggests, is a parrot who reasserts the deputy governor's idea that attacking the girls' testimony is an attempt to overthrow the court. Danforth calls for warrants for all the signatories in order to examine their motives, suggesting that they too are under suspicion.

Corey impresses Danforth with a well-written deposition attesting to Thomas Putnam's plot to gain the forfeited land of one of the condemned. When Corey refuses to give the name of the man who overheard Putnam admit his plan, Danforth dismisses the deposition.

Hale enters the argument more strongly now on the side of those who question the accusing girls' testimony. He claims that his hand was shaking "as with a wound" at the signing of Rebecca Nurse's death warrant that morning. He pleads with Danforth for lawyers to present Corey's case, but Danforth refuses. Danforth defines the dangerous and uncontrollable course he insists on following: witchcraft is an invisible crime, and there are no witnesses—only the victims can be counted upon for evidence. In effect he rules out the possibility of reasonable doubt; he argues against reason itself.

Unrelenting, Proctor presents Danforth with Mary Warren's signed statement detailing the fraud and implicating the other girls in the scheme. Abigail and the other girls are brought in for questioning. Proctor accuses Abigail of plotting murder, and Danforth is shocked. Danforth refers to Abigail as a child, and Proctor denies her this status by telling Danforth about her dancing in the woods. Hale confirms that Parris told him the story the day he arrived in Salem. Hathorne interrupts Proctor's argument by asking Mary Warren to feign a faint as she claims she did in the courtroom. She cannot, and, ironically, because she is unable to pretend a lie, she is discredited in the judges' eyes—an absolute reversal of reason.

Led by Abigail, the girls act frightened and complain of a cold wind. In turn, they accuse Mary Warren of afflicting them. Proctor insists they are pretending and calls Abigail a whore. Finally, he admits that he has "known" Abigail and that she plans to "dance with [him] on his wife's grave." Abigail indignantly refuses to answer the charge and threatens to leave if she has to hear more. Proctor says his wife is guilty of nothing but knowing a whore when she sees one.

Danforth sends for Elizabeth Proctor, who is not allowed to look at her husband or at Abigail. Not realizing that he has confessed, she lies to protect her husband and denies that he ever committed lechery. Danforth concludes that it is Proctor who has lied, but Hale recognizes Abigail's vengeance at work. To protect herself, Abigail feigns a last incident of sorcery. She says she sees a yellow bird in the rafters and charges that Mary Warren's spirit has changed its shape and is trying to tear at her face. All the girls join in to mock Mary Warren, and, as Proctor tries to comfort her, she turns on him and accuses him of being "the Devil's man." Danforth throws Proctor and Corey into jail. Hale denounces the proceedings and storms out.

Act 4 begins in what appears to be an empty jail cell. The marshall enters and wakes two sleeping prisoners, Tituba and the beggar woman. All are engaged in some form of escapist behavior: the marshall is drunk and the women seem to have lost their minds during their incarceration. They speak of the Devil carrying them off to Barbados; the marshall leads them out, clearing the cell.

Danforth sends for Parris in order to question him concerning the reappearance of Reverend Hale. There have been disruptions in the trials in the town of Andover, and Hathorne suggests Hale may have been preaching there. The marshall describes Parris's recent behavior as somewhat mad: he has been seen openly weeping in the town. We learn that the residents of Salem are becoming disgruntled: so many are in jail that there are not enough free men to tend to the crops and cattle. We learn also that Hale has returned to Salem to try to convince Rebecca Nurse and the other condemned persons to confess in order to save their lives. Parris also tells Danforth that Abigail has stolen all his savings and has run off. Parris brings up rebellious events in Andover as a possible explanation for Abigail's disappearance. All three men—especially Parris—begin to realize that the hanging of such well-respected people as Rebecca Nurse and John Proctor will bring rebellion to Salem.

Hale enters and speaks directly to Danforth: "You must pardon them. They will not budge." Danforth's response reveals his theory of justice, which is more a theory of political expediency: "I cannot pardon these when twelve are already hanged for the same crime. It is not just." Danforth brings in Elizabeth Proctor; his goal is to obtain her assistance in convincing her husband to confess. Hale, despite the frequent objections of Hathorne and Danforth, states his case plainly: if Proctor hangs, he will consider himself Proctor's murderer. He speaks the aphoristic moral of Miller's drama: ". . . cleave to no faith when faith brings blood." He argues that God will damn a liar less than one who throws the precious gift of life away for pride.

Elizabeth quietly replies that she thinks Hale's argument is the Devil's argument. More than his own life is at stake for John Proctor—and for Salem—than Hale realizes. Proctor must regain belief in his own essential goodness, and a confession by him could lead to renewed confidence in the court and the execution of others. Although Elizabeth does not promise to strive for her husband's confession, Danforth agrees to let her speak with Proctor alone—an overdue gesture toward keeping the private separate from the public domain.

Through the couple's discussion we learn that Proctor has been tortured and that Giles Corey was pressed to death; the stubborn old man would not answer the charge, and, as they laid stones on his chest he only said, "more weight." By neither confessing to nor denying the charge, he was able legally to leave his farm to his sons. Proctor says he is thinking about confessing for the sake of his sons. He says he cannot die a saint like Giles or Rebecca: ". . . let them that never lied die now to keep their souls. It is pretense for me, a vanity that will not blind God nor keep my children out of the wind." He asks for Elizabeth's opinion, but she says it is not for her to forgive him if he will not forgive himself. She is sure, though, that whatever he does "a good man does it." She confesses the results of her own soul-searching, that she has sins of her own, and that "it needs a cold wife to prompt lechery." Proctor objects, but she continues: "I counted myself so plain, so poorly made, no honest love could come to me." There is none of the tension and distance between them as was evident in Act 2.

Proctor agrees to confess, but he will not testify against Rebecca Nurse. He also refuses to sign a written statement, knowing it will be used to add credence to the court's past and future actions. Danforth discounts his oral confession, and Rebecca and Proctor are led to the gallows. Parris and Hale make a last effort to convince Elizabeth to plead with him. It is she who has the last word: "He have his goodness now. God forbid I take it from him!"

Through Elizabeth's words, Miller affirms the dangerous disorder of a society that would fuse matters of personal conscience with the public state, the inherent instability of a people that would judge the character of an individual rather than his actions. In a final note entitled "Echoes Down the Corridor," the author recounts the further activities of the historical characters, ending with the claim: ". . . to all intents and purposes, the power of theocracy in Massachusetts was broken." ❖

—*Martha Serpas*
University of Houston

List of Characters

Reverend Parris, a widower in his mid-forties, began his ministry in Salem after leaving a merchant's life in Barbados. Parris is a paranoid who is obsessed with maintaining his authority and with concealing the selfishness of his own interests. Some of the congregation may indeed have resented Parris's appointment and his fire-and-brimstone preaching. His concern with safeguarding his own position and his desire to align himself with authorities more powerful than he ensure that he supports and encourages the witch trials.

Betty Parris is Reverend Parris's ten-year-old daughter. At the opening of the play, she feigns a bizarre illness after being discovered dancing in the woods. She becomes part of the circle of girls who testify to the practice of witchcraft by others.

Tituba is Reverend Parris's slave, a native of Barbados, who is first blamed for Betty Parris's illness. Tituba says that the girls persuaded her to conjure the dead. To defend herself against charges of witchcraft, Tituba claims to have seen particular local women cavorting with the Devil. The names she lists are those suggested in questions put to her by Thomas Putnam.

Abigail Williams is the seventeen-year-old orphaned niece of Reverend Parris. Miller's stage note characterizes her as having "an endless capacity for dissembling." Her accusations begin the witch-hunt and are prompted by her efforts to conceal her own guilt; Abigail had been employed by Elizabeth and John Proctor but was dismissed when Elizabeth discovered that John and Abigail had a sexual relationship. Although Proctor spurned Abigail, she deludes herself into believing he will take her as his wife, and she schemes to have Elizabeth tried as a witch. At the play's end, she robs her uncle and runs off. The afterword, "Echoes Down the Corridor," purports her to be working as a prostitute in Boston.

Ann Putnam is the forty-five-year-old wife of Thomas Putnam. She is tormented by the infant deaths of seven of her children. Ruth, her only surviving daughter, is one of the accusing girls. Ann's grief and subsequent guilt make her quick to blame Satanic forces for the loss of her children. To Rebecca Nurse, she says, "You think it God's work you should never lose a child, nor a grandchild either, and I bury all but one? There are wheels within wheels in this village, and fires within fires!"

Thomas Putnam is the wealthiest man in the village and the husband of Ann. Late in the play, Giles Corey accuses Putnam of fueling the witch trials in order to acquire the land of those convicted. Miller's notes cite several instances of the historical Putnam's ruthless vindictiveness.

Mary Warren is the seventeen-year-old servant of Elizabeth and John Proctor. Miller's note describes her as "subservient, naive, lonely." At first loyal to Abigail Williams and the other girls, Mary is convinced by John Proctor to reveal the girls as frauds. Her weakness and lack of confidence cause her to crumble under the judges' questioning and the girls' pressure, and she reverts to her former stance as victim turned indicter.

John Proctor is a farmer in his mid-thirties. He is an indepen-dent, well-respected man in Salem. He is deeply troubled by his own guilt over his adulterous and lecherous behavior. His strong resistance to the witch trials is undermined by his fear that his own sin makes him a hypocrite. Miller uses Proctor as a vehicle for the play's major moral questions. At the end of the play, he is able to overcome his ambivalent emotions and fol-low his convictions with confidence.

Rebecca Nurse is the seventy-two-year-old wife of Francis Nurse. Salem residents hold the Nurses in the highest regard, and Rebecca is particularly admired for her works of charity. Miller's note explains that the Nurses at one time found them-selves opposed by the Putnams in a land dispute.

Giles Corey is an eighty-three-year-old opinionated and stub-born man who is often at legal odds with his neighbors, even his friend John Proctor. The innocent question that Corey puts to Hale about his wife's propensity for reading books results in her arrest for practicing witchcraft. Corey submits to death by pressing rather than answer the charge of witchcraft.

Reverend John Hale is the intellectual minister serving the near-by town of Beverly. An eager forty-year-old, Hale is delighted at being summoned to give his professional opinion in Salem.

At first impressed by his own importance and by the presence of the learned Boston judges, Hale eventually begins to doubt the credibility of the girls' testimony. As the list of condemned lengthens, Hale's own sense of guilt becomes unbearable, and he denounces the proceedings and returns to Beverly. At the play's close, he comes back to Salem and tries to convince those condemned to confess in order to save their lives.

Elizabeth Proctor is John Proctor's wife. She is the first character to make an accurate determination of Abigail's motives. She is arrested for witchcraft but is not executed because she is pregnant. She forgives John for his wrongdoing with Abigail, and late in the play she confesses to him that her own feelings of worthlessness prompted her cold attitude toward him.

Francis Nurse is the elderly husband of Rebecca Nurse and a highly regarded resident of Salem. He organizes a petition in support of his accused wife. The Nurses at one time found themselves opposed by the Putnams in a land dispute.

Ezekiel Cheever is a marshall of the court. He is dazzled by the judges' authority and eager to hand over whatever meager "evidence" he might have. He exemplifies how unquestioned obedience to authority can blind one to the truth—as illustrated by his predisposition to see Mary Warren's needle as a Satanic weapon rather than a harmless instrument used in sewing.

Judge Hathorne is a Salem judge who Miller describes as "bitter" and "remorseless." He is a zealot who supports the views of the deputy governor.

Deputy Governor Danforth is a serious man in his sixties. Miller's note describes him as having some sophistication and humor "that does not interfere with an exact loyalty to his position and his cause." His belief in the infallibility of his own moral judgment blinds him to the fraud committed by the girls. ❖

Critical Views

[Robert Warshaw (1917–1955) was an important theatre critic whose collected essays, *The Immediate
Experience: Movies, Comics, Theatre, and Other
Aspects of Popular Culture* (1964), were published
posthumously. In this extract, Warshaw asserts that
Miller's real intent in *The Crucible* was to make a political statement about American life in the 1950s.]

⟨. . .⟩ let us indeed not be misled. Mr. Miller has nothing to say
about the Salem trials and makes only the flimsiest pretense
that he has. *The Crucible* was written to say something about
Alger Hiss and Owen Lattimore, Julius and Ethel Rosenberg,
Senator McCarthy, the actors who have lost their jobs on radio
and television, in short the whole complex that is spoken of,
with a certain lowering of the voice, as the "present atmosphere." And yet not to say anything about that either, but only
to suggest that a great deal might be said, oh an infinitely
great deal, if it were not that—what? Well, perhaps if it were
not that the "present atmosphere" itself makes such plain
speaking impossible. As it is, there is nothing for it but to write
plays of "universal significance"—and, after all, that's what a
serious dramatist is supposed to do anyway.

What, then, *is* Mr. Miller trying to say to us? It's hard to tell.
In *The Crucible* innocent people are accused and convicted of
witchcraft on the most absurd testimony—in fact, the testimony of those who themselves have meddled in witchcraft and
are therefore doubly to be distrusted. Decent citizens who sign
petitions attesting to the good character of their accused
friends and neighbors are thrown into prison as suspects.
Anyone who tries to introduce into court the voice of reason is
likely to be held in contempt. One of the accused refuses to
plead and is pressed to death. No one is acquitted; the only
way out for the accused is to make false confessions and themselves join the accusers. Seeing all this on the stage, we are
free to reflect that something very like these trials has been

going on in recent years in the United States. How much like? Mr. Miller does not say. But *very* like, allowing of course for some superficial differences: no one has been pressed to death in recent years, for instance. Still, people have lost their jobs for refusing to say under oath whether or not they are Communists. The essential pattern is the same, isn't it? And when we speak of "universal significance," we mean sticking to the essential pattern, don't we? Mr. Miller is under no obligation to tell us whether he thinks the trial of Alger Hiss, let us say, was a "witch trial"; he is writing about the Salem trials.

Or, again, the play reaches its climax with John and Elizabeth Proctor facing the problem of whether John should save himself from execution by making a false confession; he elects finally to accept death, for his tormentors will not be satisfied with his mere admission of guilt: he would be required to implicate others, thus betraying his innocent friends, and his confession would of course be used to justify the hanging of the other convicted witches in the face of growing community unrest. Now it is very hard to watch this scene without thinking of Julius and Ethel Rosenberg, who might also save their lives by confessing. Does Mr. Miller believe that the only confession possible for them would be a false one, implicating innocent people? Naturally, there is no way for him to let us know; perhaps he was not even thinking of the Rosenbergs at all. How can he be held responsible for what comes into my head while I watch his play? And if I think of the Rosenbergs and somebody else thinks of Alger Hiss, and still another thinks of the Prague trial, doesn't that simply prove all over again that the play has universal significance?

—Robert Warshaw, "The Liberal Conscience in *The Crucible: Arthur Miller and His Audience*," *Commentary* 15, No. 3 (March 1953): 268–69

DAVID LEVIN ON EARLY AND MODERN WITCH HUNTS

[David Levin (b. 1924), a prolific scholar of literature and history, is the Commonwealth Professor of English at the University of Virginia. His publications include *What Happened in Salem? Pertaining to the Seventeenth-Century Witchcraft Trials* (1960), *In Defense of Historical Literature* (1967), and *Forms of Uncertainty: Essays in Historical Criticism* (1992). In this extract, Levin argues for the validity of Miller's use of seventeenth-century Salem as a metaphor for the unfair practices of anticommunist "witch hunts" of the McCarthy era.]

The Crucible dramatizes brilliantly the dilemma of an innocent man who must confess falsely if he wants to live and who finally gains the courage to insist on his innocence—and hang. To increase the impact of this final choice, Mr. Miller has filled his play with ironies. John Proctor, the fated hero, has been guilty of adultery but is too proud to confess or entirely to repent. In order to save his wife from execution by showing that her leading accuser is "a whore," he has at last brought himself to confess his adultery before the Deputy-Governor of Massachusetts Bay; but his wife, who "has never told a lie" and who has punished him severely for his infidelity, now lies to protect his name. Denying that he had been unfaithful, she convinces the court that he has lied to save her life. In the end, Proctor, reconciled with his wife and determined to live, can have his freedom if he will confess to witchcraft, a crime he has not committed.

This battery of ironies is directed against the basic objective of the play: absolute morality. In the twentieth century as well as the seventeenth, Mr. Miller insists in his preface, this construction of human pride makes devils of the opponents of orthodoxy and destroys individual freedom. Using the Salem episode to show that it also blinds people to truth, he has his characters turn the truth upside down. At the beginning of the play, the Reverend John Hale announces fatuously that he can distinguish precisely between diabolical and merely sinful actions; in the last act the remorseful Hale is trying desperately to persuade innocent convicts to confess falsely in order to avoid execution. The orthodox court, moreover, will not believe that Abigail Williams, who has falsely confessed to witchcraft, falsely denied adultery, and falsely cried out upon "witches," is "a whore"; but it is convinced that Proctor, who has told the truth about both his adultery and his innocence of witchcraft, is a witch.

What Mr. Miller considers the essential nature of the episode appears quite clearly in his play. The helplessness of an innocent defendant, the court's insistence on leaping to dubious conclusions, the jeopardy of any ordinary person who presumes to question the court's methods, the heroism of a defendant who cleaves to truth at the cost of his life, the ease with which vengeful motives can be served by a government's attempt to fight the Devil, and the disastrous aid which a self-serving confession gives injustice by encouraging the court's belief in the genuineness of the conspiracy—all this makes the play almost oppressively instructive, especially when one is watching rather than reading it. When one remembers the "invisible" nature of the crimes charged, the use of confessed conspirators against defendants who refuse to confess, the punishment of those only who insist on their innocence, then the analogy to McCarthyism seems quite valid.

—David Levin, "Salem Witchcraft in Recent Fiction and Drama," *New England Quarterly* 28, No. 4 (December 1955): 538–39

ARTHUR MILLER ON ABSOLUTE EVIL

[Arthur Miller's introduction to his *Collected Plays* (1957) allowed him to reflect on the purpose and composition of his plays. In this extract from that introduction, Miller maintains that his examination of the witch trial records led him to believe in the absolute evil of the prosecutors, a trait that Miller finds evident in his own age.]

In reading the record, which was taken down verbatim at the trial, I found one recurring note which had a growing effect upon my concept, not only of the phenomenon itself, but of our modern way of thinking about people, and especially of the treatment of evil in contemporary drama. Some critics have taken exception, for instance, to the unrelieved badness of the prosecution in my play. I understand how this is possible, and I plead no mitigation, but I was up against historical facts which were immutable. I do not think that either the record itself or the numerous commentaries upon it reveal any mitigation of the unrelieved, straightforward, and absolute dedication to evil displayed by the judges of these trials and the prosecutors. After days of study it became quite incredible how perfect they were in this respect. I recall, almost as in a dream, how Rebecca Nurse, a pious and universally respected woman of great age, was literally taken by force from her sickbed and ferociously cross-examined. No human weakness could be displayed without the prosecution's stabbing into it with greater fury. The most patent contradictions, almost laughable even in that day, were overridden with warnings not to repeat their mention. There was a sadism here that was breathtaking.

So much so, that I sought but could not at the time take hold of a concept of man which might really begin to account for such evil. For instance, it seems beyond doubt that members of the Putnam family consciously, coldly, and with malice aforethought conferred in private with some of the girls, and told them whom it was desirable to cry out upon next. There is and will always be in my mind the spectacle of the great minister, and ideological authority behind the prosecution, Cotton Mather, galloping up to the scaffold to beat back a crowd of villagers so moved by the towering dignity of the victims as to want to free them.

It was not difficult to foresee the objections to such absolute evil in men; we are committed, after all, to the belief that it does not and cannot exist. Had I this play to write now, however, I might proceed on an altered concept. I should say that my own—and the critics'—unbelief in this depth of evil is concomitant with our unbelief in good, too. I should now examine this fact of evil as such. Instead, I sought to make Danforth, for instance, perceptible as a human being by showing him somewhat put off by Mary Warren's turnabout at the height of the trials, which caused no little confusion. In my play, Danforth seems about to conceive of the truth, and surely there is a disposition in him at least to listen to arguments that go counter to the line of the prosecution. There is no such swerving in the record, and I think now, almost four years after the writing of it, that I was wrong in mitigating the evil of this man and the judges he represents. Instead, I would perfect his evil to its utmost and make an open issue, a thematic consideration of it in the play. I believe now, as I did not conceive then, that there are people dedicated to evil in the world; that without their perverse example we should not know the good. Evil is not a mistake but a fact in itself. I have never proceeded psychoanalytically in my thought, but neither have I been separated from that humane if not humanistic conception of man as being essentially innocent while the evil in him represents but a perversion of his frustrated love. I posit no metaphysical force of evil which totally possesses certain individuals, nor do I even deny that given infinite wisdom and patience and knowledge any human being can be saved from himself. I believe merely that, from whatever cause, a dedication to evil, not mistaking it for good, but knowing it as evil and loving it as evil, is possible in human beings who appear agreeable and normal. I think now that one of the hidden weaknesses of our whole approach to dramatic psychology is our inability to face this fact—to conceive, in effect, of Iago.

The Crucible is a "tough" play. My criticism of it now would be that it is not tough enough. I say this not merely out of deference to the record of these trials, but out of consideration for drama. We are so intent upon getting sympathy for our characters that the consequences of evil are being muddied by sentimentality under the guise of a temperate weighing of causes. The tranquility of the bad man lies at the heart of not only moral philosophy but dramaturgy as well. But my central intention in this play was to one side of this idea, which was realized only as the play was in production. All I sought here was to take a step not only beyond the realization of guilt, but beyond the helpless victimization of the hero.

—Arthur Miller, "Introduction," *Collected Plays* (New York: Viking Press, 1957), pp. 42–44

PAUL WEST ON THE LOSS OF HUMAN DIGNITY

[Paul West (b. 1930), a novelist, short story writer, and critic, is a professor of English at Pennsylvania State University. His publications include *The Wine of Absurdity: Essays on Life and Consolation* (1966) and *The Modern Novel* (1966). In this extract, West traces the loss of the central character's dignity as he passes through the various stages of his ordeal with an uncompassionate society.]

Miller's most shattering play is *The Crucible*. Its point is blatant: if you take a man's conscience out of his own hands, you at once deprive him of identity and of pride. We must not sell our souls to society, but we must not, cannot, separate ourselves either. We should be able to think for ourselves, express what we think, or keep it quiet. We are entitled to be fairly reported, to be protected against false informers and wild assertion. The human community in Salem, Massachusetts, failed in its responsibility to its members; so also, says Miller in his introduction, did America fail its citizens during the Macarthy purge. Of his early response to Macarthyism he writes: "It was as though the whole country had been born anew, without a memory even of certain elemental decencies which, a year or two earlier, no one would have imagined could be altered, let alone forgotten". He goes on to say how he studied the record of the Salem trial: "After days of study it became quite incredible how Rebecca Nurse, a pious and universally respected woman of great age, was literally taken by force from her sickbed and ferociously cross-examined . . . There was a sadism here that was breath-taking".

He then talks of social guilt as allied to religious mania, and explains such manifestations in terms of absolute evil: "I believe now, as I did not conceive then, that there are people dedicated to evil, . . that without their perverse example we should not know the good". *The Crucible* shows the burning-away of human decency—of humanity its very self. "It is a tough play", says Miller; "my criticism of it now would be that it is not tough enough". It is a play about depravity. No one is capable of guessing at the innermost mind of another. To guess at it in order to do him some good is tricky enough, and presumptuous. To guess at it in order to jail him or to get him hanged is monstrous.

We are shown a progress of the human soul. An action that begins with hysterical accusations eventually breaks into an awful calm in which some one can get up and say: "We've hanged a dozen people already; now, of course, we might seem to be wrong; but it would not be fair to the hanged if we spared the rest of the condemned". Institutions, says Miller, easily become dehumanised; we acquire habits, and soon the habits acquire us. What is most frightening and sickening in this play is the spectacle of once reasonable human beings in the act of rationalising their loss of charity, their discarding of good sense. Excess, as Camus has said, maintains its place in man's heart; murder and loneliness often go together. Everyman must strive to avoid the indifference which habit brings. A constant and fresh response to other lives is the only way to justify pride in being human.

—Paul West, "Arthur Miller and the Human Mice," *Hibbert Journal* No. 241 (January 1963): 85

SHEILA HUFTEL ON THE TIMELESS MESSAGE OF *THE CRUCIBLE*

[Sheila Huftel is a critic of drama and literature and author of *Arthur Miller: The Burning Glass* (1965), from which the following extract is taken. Here, Huftel points out the universal nature of the conflicts in *The Crucible* and warns against a too restrictive political interpretation of the play.]

The scope of *The Crucible* is wide; a general illustration of a witch-hunt and an explanation of how and why they break out. To limit it to one particular twentieth-century witch-hunt is to wear blinkers. Miller's comment is for yesterday as well as for the day after tomorrow, and not merely the here-and-now of American politics. It is surely a kind of vanity to corner-off a section of a large work, identify with it, and claim that as the subject of the whole. It cannot be overlooked that *The Crucible* is applicable to any situation that allows the accuser to be always holy, as it also is to any confict between the individual and authority. Timeless as *An Enemy of the People,* it symbolizes all forms of heresy-hunting, religious and political.

Miller himself covers the whole field by discussing contemporary diabolism alongside Hale's belief in the Devil. He writes of the necessity of the Devil: "A weapon designed and used time and time again in every age to whip men into a surrender to a particular church or church-state." He traces the Devil's progress, from Lucifer of the Spanish Inquisition to current politics. "A political policy is equated with moral right, and opposition to it with diabolical malevolence. Once such an equation is effectively made, society becomes a congerie of plots and counterplots, and the main role of government changes from that of the arbiter to that of the scourge of God."

In answer to the criticism, and much has been made of it, that witches are an impossibility whereas Communists are a fact, Miller writes that he has no doubt people were communing with the devil in Salem. He cites as evidence Tituba's confession and the behavior of the children who were known to have indulged in sorceries. It was, incidentally, a cardinal fault in Sartre's film of the play, *Les Sorciers de Salem,* that, not believing in witches himself, he allowed none of his characters to believe in them. This uncompromising twentieth-century attitude not only robbed the film of conviction, but of an important seventeenth-century viewpoint that should have been its concern.

It may be that I have a simple mind. But if a dramatist says his play deals with the Salem witch-hunt and goes to the length of writing about it, I am inclined to believe him. By implication the play would be about general witch-hunting and by inference about McCarthyism, which happened to be the current witch-hunt. I believe the play has been distorted by trying to link the two too closely. But some American critics found the link not close enough, and charged Miller with evasion. To ignore their objections would be evasive. I admit that their greater involvement would make them more sensitive to this aspect of the play; it might also lead them to a greater prejudice.

—Sheila Huftel, *Arthur Miller: The Burning Glass* (Secaucus, NJ: Citadel Press, 1965), pp. 133–34

JEAN GOULD ON THE EARLY PRODUCTIONS OF *THE CRUCIBLE*

[Jean Gould (1909–1993) was an important critic of American literature. Her works include *Robert Frost: The Aim Was Song* (1965), *Amy: The World of Amy Lowell and the Imagist Movement* (1975), and *American Women Poets: Pioneers of Modern Poetry* (1980). In this extract from her book on American drama, Gould notes Miller's dissatisfaction with the first production of *The Crucible* and how he revised the work and staged it himself.]

The Crucible had two opening nights of two separate productions six months apart, one in January and one in July of 1953. The first was staged with full sets by Jed Harris, and came close to being a flop because of the rigidity of the production. The analogy was clear enough, the preachment powerful, but the play was considered heavy-handed, lacking in the warmth or passion necessary for good drama. Even a fine actor like Arthur Kennedy (who had scored as Biff, the older son, along with Lee Cobb, as Willy Loman, in *Salesman*) seemed wooden in the role of John Proctor, the chief protagonist in *The Crucible*. The playwright was deeply distressed by the reactions of critics and audiences to the play, whose subject he considered of the gravest import. He determined to keep his work before the public, to keep his message alive. He decided to stage it himself, adding a single scene between Proctor and Abigail (leader of the accusers) to heighten the passion and strengthen the motivation. In his production he did away with the scenery, using drapes as a backdrop to the action as well as an effectively lit cyclorama, which gave more flexibility and fluency to his interpretation of history. It pointed up the timelessness of the tragic situation in the play, the implication that, regardless of the century in which it occurs, "the sin of public terror is that it divests man of conscience, of himself."

The revised production, which had a long run in the Martin Beck Theatre before going on a national tour, came much closer to evoking the response Miller had anticipated. Audiences were deeply stirred, and critics agreed that the new version had greater dramatic and artistic value than before. If his drama did not reach the heights of true tragedy, it elevated the emotional plane of plays possessing "broad social awareness," to use the playwright's term. (His reply to the critics about the lack of warmth in the work was that in such plays emotion and private feeling should be restrained. In the second production, however, the checkrein was not so much in evidence, and as a result, the play was far more effective.)

—Jean Gould, *Modern American Playwrights* (New York: Dodd, Mead, 1966), pp. 254–55

STEPHEN FENDER ON MILLER'S USE OF LANGUAGE IN *THE CRUCIBLE*

[Stephen Fender is the author of many books, including *Plotting the Golden West: American Literature and the Rhetoric of the California Trail* (1981) and *Sea Changes: British Emigration and American Literature* (1992). In this extract, Fender argues that Miller's reproduction of Puritan speech patterns not only enhances the conflict between the individual and society but becomes part of the play's subject.]

So, far from having a 'higher self-awareness', as Miller thought, the American Puritans were undecided about how much importance to give to specific human acts: good works may or may not proceed from a state of grace; all that was certain was that nothing was what it seemed; the concrete fact had no assured validity. But what Miller has caught so successfully, despite his theory, is the peculiar way in which the Puritans spoke whenever they talked about sin. One can say even more than that: Miller has, in fact, made the fullest dramatic use of the language, using its peculiarities to limit the characters speaking it and even making it part of the play's subject.

The language plays its part, for example, in establishing the rather complex ironic structure in the scene in which the Reverend Hale first appears. Betty is lying ill, and Parris, secretly fearing that she might be affected by witchcraft, has called in an expert in detecting witchcraft. The situation itself is ironic; it is a measure of his own confusion about Betty that Parris must call in an expert with weighty volumes under his arm to tell him what to think about his daughter's exhaustion and shock. The audience also suspects that Parris depends on Hale's authority as a compensation for being unable to deal with Abigail. Another aspect of the irony is that the audience knows the expert's opinion will change nothing; the Putnams and the other townspeople—even Parris himself—have now convinced themselves that witchcraft is to blame. Finally, of course, the audience has already been given enough evidence—in the hasty conference between Abigail, Betty and Mary Warren and in Abigail's plea to Proctor—that Hale's knowledge of witchcraft is irrelevant to the situation. ⟨. . .⟩

Proctor must indeed cast off the terminology of Salem. But what he is rejecting is not a monolithic system, not a 'coherently worked-out philosophy'. Salem speech is 'articulate' in only a very limited sense of the word; 'voluble' or 'smooth' would apply more aptly. One needs to make this point because our response to the play is more complex than it would be if Proctor were a modern existential hero working out his own solution in opposition to the conventions of society. Salem has no conventions. Its evil is not positive. Its ethics are not wrong; they are non-existent. What makes the progress of the witch-hunt so terrifying for the audience is the realization that the trial has no programme. If Proctor and the others were being tested—and found wanting—according to a wrong-headed but consistent set of values, our reaction to the play would be quite different. What terrifies us is that we never know from what direction the next attack will come, and we are struck more by what Miller, in his introduction to the *Collected Plays,* calls 'the swirling and ludicrous mysticism [elevated] to a level of high moral debate' of the characters than we are by their 'moral awareness'. John Proctor acts not as a rebel but as the restorer of what the audience take to be normal human values. What Miller actually achieved in *The Crucible* is far more important than what he apparently feels guilty for not having achieved.

> —Stephen Fender, "Precision and Pseudo Precision in *The Crucible," Journal of American Studies* 1, No. 1 (April 1967): 94, 98

EDWARD MURRAY ON THE FUSION OF THE PERSONAL AND THE SOCIAL IN *THE CRUCIBLE*

[Edward Murray (b. 1928) is a film and theatre critic who has written *The Cinematic Imagination* (1972), *Fellini: The Artist* (1976), and *Varieties of Dramatic Structure* (1990). In this extract from his book on Miller, Murray believes that *The Crucible* represents a successful fusion of the personal and the social in its depiction of the emotional conflicts of the major characters.]

Granting, it might be objected, that *Crucible* contains more variety than is usually allowed for it, is it not true that it remains a bit too simple? For some readers, the neatness of the thematic spectrum is perhaps an argument against the play's complexity, and for those who demand shading, not among multiple points of view but in each individual character, Miller's play is unsatisfactory. The same readers may also feel that Proctor's infidelity is not enough of a complication, that it is too flimsy a foundation on which to erect the structure of *Crucible.* The crucial question, however, is: Does Miller succeed in fusing the "personal" and the "social"? A close reading of the play would suggest that he does. A flaw in Proctor's marriage allows the trials to materialize; no act—even the most intimate of sexual relations—would seem isolated from the "social." Elizabeth admits to being "cold"; but it is not due to being "puritanical," as some critics would have it, or to "lack of love"; she says (as I have quoted previously): "John, I counted myself so plain, so poorly made, no honest love could come to me! . . . I never knew how I should say my love." John asks: "Is the accuser always holy now?" This has both a "personal" and a "social" reference; "personal" because Elizabeth accuses John of evil and she is not "holy" (although she admits her faults later), while John himself learns that he is not as "holy" as he had thought; "social" because, to take but one instance, Abigail and the girls are not "holy" but they accuse others. This much is fairly obvious. ⟨. . .⟩ Miller *intended* to focus on "that guilt residing in Salem which the hysteria merely unleashed" ("Introduction"). Is it necessary that the guilt be of a single kind? Is it not possible—indeed probable—that various kinds of guilt may come to focus upon a single "social" situation? Of course, Elizabeth admits to keeping a "cold house"; and Salem is a "cold" community; and the activity of the girls in the woods suggests sexual repression—but this is far from being the entire explanation of events. And, as Miller *dramatizes* his material, guilt is not the sole motive for the trials. Nor would it seem either necessary or desirable that it should be in order to link the "personal" to the "social." Some critics want a single explanation for the "enemy"; but certainly the interest of the play, for a mature reader, is that the "enemy" assumes many shapes and refuses to be reduced to a single motivation. Mrs. Putnam is filled with hate because she lost seven babies at birth; Mr. Putnam wants land; Parris wants to protect his job; Tituba wants to save her neck; Abigail wants John—and so it goes. If it be objected that few of these characters seem genuinely convinced of witchcraft, that would seem to be more of an historical than an aesthetic question. Miller, it must be owned, exposed himself to such criticism by identifying his play with a specific period. It is certainly arguable whether we get, as Miller says we do, the "essential nature" of the Salem trials; but no matter—what we do get is an extremely effective drama. Yet, even from the merely "historical" standpoint, Miller has complicated his action; for example, and this is to the modern taste, Betty appears to be suffering from some kind of self-damaging guilt complex brought about from the previous night's outing in the woods; but there is a nice question how much Abigail and the girls really believe in witchcraft. Although Abigail tells Parris and John that it was just a "sport," she *did* drink chicken blood as a charm to kill Elizabeth, which suggests that Miller has mixed various kinds of motives to propel his action.

Intrinsically, *The Crucible* is complex, coherent, and convincing; that is, it succeeds *as a play* on its own premises and merits. Although one might hesitate to agree that *The Crucible* is superior to *Death of a Salesman*—it seems to lack the sensuousness, the imaginative and technical brilliance, even the warm humanity, of the earlier play—still it remains one of Miller's best plays and one of the most impressive achievements of the American theater.

—Edward Murray, *Arthur Miller: Dramatist* (New York: Ungar, 1967), pp. 73–75

LEONARD MOSS ON ARTHUR MILLER'S POLITICAL
DIFFICULTIES AFTER WRITING *THE CRUCIBLE*

[Leonard Moss (b. 1931), a former professor of comparative literature at State University of New York College in Geneseo, is the author of *Arthur Miller* (1967), from which the following extract is taken. Here, Moss relates how *The Crucible* was written as an attack on contemporary threats to free expression but that the play itself caused Miller himself to come under suspicion as a subversive.]

During the Depression and war, Miller had been inspired by liberal reform programs designed to improve conditions in business, politics, and the arts. After the war he participated in those programs more actively. The situation in the theater particularly disturbed him: he saw a threat to free expression emerging that superseded "commercialization." "I may be wrong," he said, "but I sense that the playwrights have become more timid with experience and maturity, timid in ethical and social idea, theatrical method, and stylistic means. . . . We have an atmosphere of dread, an . . . accepted party line, a sanctified complex of moods and attitudes, proper and improper."

This "atmosphere of dread" Miller ascribed in part to the inquiries concerning disloyalty then being conducted by certain federal agencies and Congressional committees. He believed that these investigations were planned to harass those with unpopular political views. He therefore wrote *The Crucible* to expose the process by which "terror . . . was being knowingly planned and consciously engineered. . . . Above all, above all horrors, I saw accepted the notion that conscience was no longer a private matter but one of state administration." He was not referring to any specific instance or individual—such as Senator Joseph McCarthy, considered by many to be the most brutal of the official interrogators; instead, he was "trying to tell people that the great 'issues' which the hysteria was allegedly about" in colonial as well as in contemporary America "were covers for petty ambitions, hardheaded political drives, and the fantasies of very small and vengeful minds."

Then the playwright became a principal in the debate rather than merely a witness for the defense. Ironically, state authorities, by insisting that he inform on others and confess sins against the community, presented him with a challenge to "conscience" directly analogous to that which had confronted the protagonist of *The Crucible*. In the play he had articulated his faith in the ability of the free individual to withstand irrational social pressures and to determine positive standards of citizenship. Now he demonstrated his faith through his conduct.

In March, 1954, the State Department refused Miller a passport to visit Brussels for the Belgian première of *The Crucible*. His application was "rejected under regulations denying passports to persons believed to be supporting the Communist movement, whether or not they are members of the

Communist party." Miller indignantly denied "suppporting any Communist movement"; on July 3, he published a satire on the loyalty mania, patterned after Swift's "Modest Proposal," in which he sarcastically proposed formal specifications for judging treason that would be consistent with the policies he felt were actually operative. Among other things, it would be punishable to have "engaged in Conversations, talks, public or private meetings, lectures, visits, or communications, the nature of which is not illegal but on the other hand not Positively Conducive to the Defence of the Nation against the Enemy."
  —Leonard Moss, *Arthur Miller* (New York: Twayne, 1967), pp. 26–28

❖

BENJAMIN NELSON ON *THE CRUCIBLE* AS A DEPICTION OF CORPORATE HYSTERIA

[Benjamin Nelson (b. 1935), a professor of English at Fairleigh Dickinson University, is the author of *Tennessee Williams: The Man and His Work* (1961) and *Arthur Miller: Portrait of a Playwright* (1970), from which the following extract is taken. Here, Nelson shows how Miller found in the people of seventeenth-century Salem an ideal example of corporate or communal hysteria.]

Undoubtedly *The Crucible* was inspired by the social and political climate of the United States in the 1950s. Miller was the first to make this admission. Although he never claimed that McCarthyism was a literal resurrection of the Salem witchhunts—Communists after all have a higher degree of corporeality than witches—he openly acknowledged that his reading of the court records was colored by the contemporary experience, and that he found in the transcripts pretty much what he was looking for. Still, it is infinitely too simple to suppose that because a work is influenced by something, it cannot encompass more than the particular stimulus which inspired it. It is hardly accidental that as the McCarthy fervor has waned, critical response to *The Crucible* has grown appreciably favorable. Scarcely the result of the few dialogue changes Miller subsequently made, it is in all probability the consequence of judgments based upon the play's genuine qualities rather than upon its political pertinency. *The Crucible* is topical. However, it is as pertinent to Inquisitorial Spain, the France of Robespierre and Danton, Nazi Germany, and Stalinist Russia as it is to McCarthyite America. Not to mention Salem, Massachusetts of 1692.

But if *The Crucible* is not a contemporary political allegory, neither is it an historical narrative. It is a dramatic exploration of the conditions of corporate hysteria. For all its adherence to history, the play is poetry, self-contained and defined by its aesthetic framework, and as such it ultimately stands or falls. Consequently its validity is no more dependent upon its complete fidelity to the Puritan theocracy than *Julius Caesar* and *Saint Joan* are to their historical antecedents.

Miller was neither re-creating all the particulars of the witch trials nor camouflaging current events when he chose Salem as the location for his drama. He was seeking perspective. He viewed the trails not as an isolated historical phenomenon but as part of a continuing tragedy, not exclusively Salem's child nor the twentieth century's, yet claiming kinship to each.

The playwright was particularly fascinated by the people of Salem. Because of their characters and the historical situation in which they found themselves, they possessed the moral consciousness which he wanted to dramatize. For good or ill, they were individuals who were supremely aware of the nature of their struggle. ⟨. . .⟩

Not only was their awareness razor sharp and diamond hard, but their power of articulation was eloquent. Thus, by choosing the Salemites for his subject, Miller could circumvent the dilemma which had confronted him in his previous works: the inadequacy of the modern realistic hero's dialogue to convey his consciousness. He had explored what he termed the 'subjective world' in *Death of a Salesman,* and now he wanted to create a more conscious and intelligible protagonist. The Puritans afforded him the opportunity. ⟨. . .⟩

Still another reason for Miller's choice of the historical context for his play was inherent in the structure of the Puritan theocracy. Its religion stressed the innate bestiality of man and his singular inability to remedy this woeful state. And since the source of man's depravity was the flesh, which linked him to the organic world and provided a constant source of temptation, the individual's—and society's—primary struggle was against this enticement, which was credited to the devil and which had to be resisted by constant and obsessive vigilance.

Miller also took note of the socio-political aspects of the theocracy. Although as the ruling orthodoxy of its time it still demanded an intense commitment from its members, by the final decade of the seventeenth century, the theocracy was being badly strained by a number of socially disruptive pressures. From within, the Puritan codes were no longer as binding to a new generation as they had been to previous generations who had relied on their discipline to see them through a rigorous existence in a new and harsh land. From without, land titles were in dispute in Salem because of edicts from Boston and London, and the community was unsure of its future, increasingly fearful and beset by mounting anxiety.

Given then a morbid religion, in a geographical setting of continual hardship and danger, a social climate of spiraling bewilderment and fear, and a psychological atmosphere of repression and guilt among people predisposed to blaming Satanic stimuli for unexplained phenomena, there is little wonder that even the most petty motivations and circumstances could engender a terror that would rapidly paralyze all common sense and reason.

—Benjamin Nelson, *Arthur Miller: Portrait of Playwright* (New York: David McKay Co., 1970), pp. 150–53

CHADWICK HANSEN ON TITUBA AS A METAPHORICAL BLACK WOMAN

[Chadwick Hansen (b. 1926) is an historian who has written *Witchcraft at Salem* (1969) as well as several studies of jazz music. In this extract, Hansen notes how frequently the West Indian slave Tituba has been assumed to be a black woman in various literary works, including *The Crucible*. In Hansen's view, Miller's portrayal is meant to emphasize her evil characteristics.]

The last vestige of Tituba's actual race withered away in Arthur Miller's play, *The Crucible,* leaving her a "Negro slave." And in Miller Tituba's magic is blacker as well as her race. Starkey had been appropriately vague about the magic she attributed to Tituba, calling it "tricks and spells, fragments of something like voodoo remembered from the Barbados." Miller is much more specific. His Tituba has been chanting over a boiling kettle containing, among other things, a live frog, while the girls of Salem Village dance, one of them naked, in the dark forest. And she has given one girl chicken blood to drink, as a potion with which to kill the wife of the man with whom this girl is in love. The chanting, the witch's brew, and the naked dancing in the forest are more easily attributed to Miller's unfortunate penchant for melodrama than to any specific system of magic, but the sacrificial chicken is, of course, a prominent feature of voodoo ceremony.

Miller has two dramatic reasons for blackening Tituba. One is to dramatize her as a voodoo priestess. The other will require some explanation. Miller holds the New England clergy responsible for the events at Salem; in *The Crucible* they use the witchcraft to play on the emotions of the public in a vain attempt to support their own ebbing power. Tituba was the first confessor. So in the climactic scene of his first act, Miller has a clergyman, John Hale, bring Tituba to confess to witchcraft precisely as a revivalist would bring a sinner to confess her sins.

"Now in God's holy name—" Hale begins, and Tituba responds, "Bless Him. Bless Him." A stage direction tells us that she "is rocking on her knees, sobbing in terror." The statement and response pattern continues between Hale and Tituba, as do her weeping and rocking; emotions rise until Tituba confesses; she is joined by her troupe of adolescent girls, who in the process of confessing accuse people of witchcraft as fast as they can name them, while Hale "is shouting a prayer of thanksgiving." It is as vulgar a scene as Miller ever wrote, with Tituba featured as Aunt Jemima at the Salem Camp Meeting.

—Chadwick Hansen, "The Metamorphosis of Tituba, or Why American Intellectuals Can't Tell an Indian Witch from a Negro," *New England Quarterly* 47, No. 1 (March 1974): 10–11

ORM ÖVERLAND ON MILLER'S UNWISE ADDITIONS TO *THE CRUCIBLE*

[Orm Överland (b. 1935), a critic and translator, has translated *Johan Schroder's Travels in Canada, 1863* (1989). In this extract, Överland criticizes the additions Miller made to the original version of *The Crucible,* stating that they result in needless repetition and reflect Miller's disinclination to let the play speak for itself.]

Miller's reluctance to let a play speak for itself became even more evident in his two attempts to add extra material to the original text of *The Crucible* after its first production in 1953. The first of these additions, a second scene in Act Two, helps to explain Abigail's behavior in Act Three, but, as Laurence Olivier told the playwright, it is not necessary. Although Abigail's psychotic character is brought out entirely in action and dialogue, in an encounter with John Proctor on the eve of the trial, and there is no suggestion of extra-dramatic exposition, the added scene is nevertheless evidence of Miller's sense of not having succeeded in making himself understood in the original version of the play.

More striking is the evidence provided by the series of non-dramatic interpolated passages in the first act, where the playwright takes on the roles of historian, novelist and literary critic, often all at once, speaking himself *ex cathedra* rather than through his characters *ex scena.* There is an obvious difference in intent as well as effect in writing an introductory essay to one's play and writing a series of comments that are incorporated in the text itself. The material used need not be different. For example, some of the comments on Danforth in the "Introduction" to the *Collected Plays* are quite similar to those on Parris or Hale incorporated in the play. In the one instance, however, he is looking at his play from the outside, as one of its many critics, in the other he has added new material to the play and has thus changed the text.

In effect the play has a narrator, not realized as a character but present as a voice commenting on the characters and the action and making clear some of the moral implications for the reader/audience. The director of the 1958 Off Broadway revival of *The Crucible* drew the consequences of the revised text and introduced "a narrator, called The Reader, to set the scenes and give the historical background of the play." Besides his function as one of the minor characters, this is what Alfieri does in *A View from the Bridge.* The introduction of a "narrator" element in *The Crucible* is closely related to Miller's attempts to have a separate voice present the author's view of the "generalized significance" of the "action" in the later play.

The interpolated expository passages of *The Crucible* serve two different purposes. Frequently the comments on a character merely repeat points made in that part of the drama which may be acted on the stage. Indeed, the opening words of the following paragraph on John Proctor are suggestive of the Victorian novelist guiding his readers through his story, making sure that no point, however obvious, may be missed:

> But as we shall see, the steady manner he displays does not spring from an untroubled soul. He is a sinner, a sinner not only against the moral fashion of the time, but against his own vision of decent conduct. These people had no ritual for the washing away of sins. It is another trait we inherited from them, and it has helped to discipline us as well as to breed hypocrisy among us. Proctor, respected and even feared in Salem, has come to regard himself as a kind of fraud. But no hint of this has yet appeared on the surface, and as he enters from the crowded parlor below it is a man in his prime we see, with a quiet confi-

dence and an unexpressed, hidden force. Mary Warren, his servant, can barely speak for embarrassment and fear.

Proctor's sense of guilt is central to any understanding of him as a dramatic character, but certainly this is made sufficiently clear by, for instance, the several explicit remarks made by Elizabeth as well as by his behavior on the stage.

While such passages are further instances of Miller's apparent distrust of his medium as a means of communication, other passages speak of an impatience with the limitations of the dramatic form. Miller had researched this play thoroughly, and it is as if on second thought he has regretted that he had not been able to bring as much of his research and his historical insights into the play as he would have liked. But when he in the interpolated passages takes on the roles of historian and biographer he tends to confuse the sharp line that must be drawn between the characters in a play called *The Crucible* and a group of late seventeenth century individuals bearing the same names as these characters. Thus, in the first of the two paragraphs that serve to introduce Proctor as he enters on the stage, Miller tells us:

> Proctor was a farmer in his middle thirties. He need not have been a partisan of any faction in the town, but there is evidence to suggest that he had a sharp and biting way with hypocrites. He was the kind of man—powerful of body, even-tempered, and not easily led—who cannot refuse support to partisans without drawing their deepest resentment. In Proctor's presence a fool felt his foolishness instantly—and a Proctor is always marked for calumny therefore.

The change in tense in the paragraph that follows (quoted above) suggests that Miller had a different Proctor in mind in each paragraph: the historical Proctor and the character in the play. This confusion runs through the various character sketches or brief essays on for instance Parris, Putnam and Rebecca and Francis Nurse. It should further be noted that these interpolated expository passages are often concerned with motivation, and that both psychological, religious and socio-economic explanations of the trials are given. While the information is interesting in itself and throws light on the Salem trials, it cannot add to our understanding of the drama as acted on the stage.

Whatever needs to be known about these characters and their motives by the audience must be expressed in action and dialogue. That is, if we do not accept the dichotomy of "action" and "significance," with the latter element presented by a representative of the author, a "Reader" or a narrator.

—Orm Överland, "The Action and Its Significance: Arthur Miller's Struggle with Dramatic Form," *Modern Drama* 18, No. 1 (March 1975): 6–8

C. W. E. Bigsby on Tyranny in *The Crucible*

[C. W. E. Bigsby (b. 1941) is one of the foremost critics of modern drama. He is a professor of American literature at the University of East Anglia (Norwich, England) and has written monographs on Edward Albee (1969), Tom Stoppard (1976), Joe Orton (1982), and David Mamet (1985), and several other general studies of drama. In this extract, Bigsby examines Miller's use of John Proctor as a sympathetic opponent of political oppression.]

Miller was clearly interested in the question of authority and the need to define oneself in terms of opposition of that authority, but equally clearly, despite his early espousal of Marxism, he did not look for a solution so much in communal action as in the assumption of a total responsibility for one's actions, in the restoration of the significance of the individual. For, to him, the power of authority ultimately derives from the individual's willing acquiescence in the idea of his own insignificance. He had come to feel that the 'steady and methodical inculcation into humanity of the idea of man's worthlessness—until redeemed' was the basis of all power, religious and political. It was a power which could only be broken by reasserting that significance. Thus Proctor announces, 'I like not the smell of this "authority" ', believing by that that it is possible for the individual to abstract himself from the world in which that authority has power. The process of the play, however, proves otherwise; it constitutes a moral education in the nature of power, the central significance of guilt, and, almost paradoxically, the possibility of rational analysis. Even confronted with an outbreak of irrational behaviour, Miller seeks, not wholly successfully, to impose a rational explanation. For to concede a place to the truly arbitrary and to acknowledge the authority of mystery and unmotivated action is to conceive of a world in which no moral demand can be made and no responsibility assigned. Hence, Abigail informs against Elizabeth Proctor out of jealousy, as all the girls accuse others in order to secure their own freedom. The other accusers are motivated by guilt. One of the principal changes that Miller made in dramatising the events was to raise the age of the children, thereby injecting a sexual motivation into their actions and providing an explanation for Proctor's equivocation. The sexual component, which Miller probably correctly identifies as a vital element in Puritan repressions and the consequent explosions of Dionysian rituals, becomes the fulcrum of the play. It is a dramatic strategy which is not without its distracting force, but Miller clearly sees in sexual betrayal an image of the egotism which is at the root of human cruelties and the collapse of communal values (in contrast to the element of sacrifice and selflessness evident in genuine love).

And yet he does posit the existence of an evil which exists almost in pure form. For this he offers no explanation. For all his closeness to McCarthyism and his full awareness of the atrocities of the holocaust there persisted an area of experience which resisted analysis. Thus the judges remain virtually unexamined, while the minor, though crucial figures (Parris and Hale) are presented as being motivated by considerations of career and self-importance. The principal figures, in terms of authority, Deputy-Governor Danforth and Judge Hathorne, are presented only in externals. So, though the injection of the sexual component provides a clear line of motivation for the accusers and the source of a vital sense of guilt, it does little to penetrate the evil which really fascinated him. That evil becomes simply an implacable force against which the individual defines himself. It is the bland face of administrative efficiency for which questions of moral truth are irrelevant. Indeed, later he was to regret not making Danforth more completely committed to evil:

> I was wrong in mitigating the evil of this man and the judges he represents. Instead, I would perfect his evil to its utmost and make an open issue, a thematic consideration of it in the play. I believe now, as I did not conceive then, that there are people dedicated to evil in the world; that without their perverse example we should not know the good. Evil is not a mistake but a fact in itself . . . a dedication to evil, not mistaking it for good but knowing it as evil and loving it as evil, is possible in human beings who appear agreeable and normal. I think now that one of the hidden weaknesses of our whole approach to dramatic psychology is our inability to face this fact.

It was, perhaps, a conviction having rather more to do with the painful truths of the holocaust than the realities of Puritan New England, though Miller has insisted that he found no mitigation from the unredeemed and absolute 'dedication to evil' displayed by the judges. But Miller had seen much the same force operating in the Greek theatre. Thus *Oedipus* was concerned with 'the irony of authority seeking evil outside of itself when evil is right in it, in the authority'. The problem, as he explained, was that 'I couldn't find a space, so to speak, around that evil, a space on which to stand'. The fact is that Miller seems content to register the opacity of that force. Thus Danforth is portrayed as naive, while Hathorne's intransigent blood-lust provides only a constant background rhythm to the drama which is played out in his court. There is little in the play that suggests where the blood-lust derives from. He does not propose a model of human nature which offers to explain their central role, as that of the other characters is rationalised by material or sexual jealousies and compounded by a desire to sustain one's own innocence by accusing others. Though there clearly comes a time when they must realise their own complicity in the events, and hence become the more implacable in order to conceal their sense of guilt, Miller never really explains the force which makes them such rigorous persecutors in the first place and this, I suspect, is not unconnected with the difficulty he has in establishing the precise nature of the religious fervour of late seventeenth-century New England. John Proctor's sensibility is too close to our own not to make his

judgements seem the touchstone by which to convict the prosecutors of judicious tyranny.

—C. W. E. Bigsby, *A Critical Introduction to Twentieth-Century American Drama, Volume II: Tennessee Williams, Arthur Miller, Edward Albee* (Cambridge: Cambridge University Press, 1984), pp. 194–96

E. MILLER BUDICK ON MILLER'S USE OF HISTORICAL FICTION

[E. Miller Budick is the author of *Emily Dickinson and the Life of Language* (1985), *Fiction and Historical Consciousness* (1989), and *Engendering Romance: Women Writers and the Hawthorne Tradition* (1994). In the following extract, Budick studies Miller's use of historical fiction in *The Crucible* to emphasize the distinc-
tion between fact and fiction, the subjective and the objective, in human life.]

By writing a historical drama, Miller is asking us to turn to the historical record in order to understand the ambiguous and changing nature of morality. He is evoking our sympathies for characters whose world-view and beliefs are totally different from our own, thus enabling us to do precisely what the Puritans themselves were unable to do—to accept the diversity of opinions, the variety of perceptions, the mixture of bad and good which characterize the human community.

Above all, however, Miller is making a statement about the relationship between objective fact and subjective fiction, or rather, about the existence of subjective fiction within objective fact and vice versa. *The Crucible* not only emphasizes the importance of sympathy in human relationships, but explores why sympathy must be a component of those relationships, not only if we are to see morally, but if we are to see at all. For historical fiction has the unique advantage of insisting upon the realness of the world with which it deals fictively, while simultaneously acknowledging that the world which it is now representing is a consequence as much of the readers' or viewers' subjective perceptions as of any objective fact or reality. In historical drama, the paradoxical relationship between fancy and fact is even more vivid than in written fiction, for the realness of actors enacting a history which has been fictionalized and put on the stage has, from Shakespeare on, inevitably raised its own theoretical arguments about the world and the play. "No one can really know what their lives were like," Miller begins the play. And yet he proceeds to convince us of exactly what their lives were like, as they themselves confronted what was knowable and unknowable, what was fact and fiction, in life itself.

In the case of a historical drama on the Salem witchcraft trials, the historical and literary interest found a coincidence of purpose and meaning that was startling in the extreme. For the issue of the witchcraft trials is precisely the question of the proportion of fiction to fact in our perceptions of the world; and the lesson is what can happen when individuals forget the limits of their own optical and moral senses, and fail to sympathize with fellow citizens suffering from the same impossibility of separating the imaginary from the real. Furthermore, by casting upon his contemporary audience the spectre of Salem, and pretending that Salem is contemporary America, Miller is asking us to recognize the elements of self within our projections of the devil, the subjectivity which ever colours our knowledge of the objective world.

The Crucible, then, by the very procedures which define its dramatic art, enforces upon us a recognition of the difficulty of distinguishing between the subjective and the objective, between the spectre and the witch. Hence, the play invokes our sympathy for the actors of a tragedy who viewed their lives from much the same complicated perspective by which an audience views a play. The play, in other words, imitates the situation of the Puritans, who witnessed their world as the unfolding of a drama in which external events represented internal realities. But whereas the Puritans failed to recognize the fictionality of that dramatic performance in which their lives consisted, Miller's play, as a play, enforces our awareness of the fiction. It insists that life (i.e., history) and literature are both spectres of consciousness, ours or someone else's, projections of the imagination. The Puritans' principal failing, as it emerges in the play, was their inability to accord to each other, even to themselves, the privacy and individuality which are not simply human rights but inherent features of perception itself. By extending our imaginations over centuries of difference, by identifying with the ghosts which are the past and the ghosts in which the past itself believed, we attain to the sympathetic imaginations, the spiritual charity, which the Puritans could not achieve.

> —E. Miller Budick, "History and Other Spectres in Arthur Miller's *The Crucible*," *Modern Drama* 28, No. 4 (December 1985): 549–50

❖

EDMUND S. MORGAN ON THE HISTORICITY OF *THE CRUCIBLE*

[Edmund S. Morgan (b. 1916), Sterling Professor of History at Yale University, is one of the most respected of American historians and author of several studies of Puritanism, including *The Puritan Family* (1944), *The Puritan Dilemma: The Story of John Winthrop* (1958), and *Visible Saints: The History of a Puritan Idea* (1963). In this extract, Morgan believes that Miller in *The Crucible* exhibits a faulty understanding of Puritanism but that his play's emphasis on other human values redeems it.]

A knowledge of Puritanism can help us to penetrate behind the mask that disguises some of the characters in *The Crucible* and obscures the forces at work in the Salem tragedy. Arthur Miller knew his characters well enough as human beings so that they are never concealed from him by his faulty image of Puritanism. But he does not know them as Puritans. Too often their humanity is revealed as something at odds with Puritanism. We need to understand that their Puritanism was not really at issue in the tragedy. Insofar as it entered, it affected protagonist and antagonist alike. It conceals the issue to make Samuel Parris wear the mask of Puritanism and John Proctor stand like some nineteenth-century Yankee populist thrust back into Cotton Mather's court. Parris and Proctor were both Puritans and both men. We should not look on Proctor's refusal to confess as a triumph of man over Puritan. It was a triumph of man over man and of Puritan over Puritan. Elizabeth Proctor was a Puritan and a woman; we should not see her as a Puritan when she is cold to her husband and a woman when she is warm.

In other words, the profounder implications of the action in the play are darkened by a partial identification of the antagonist as Puritanism. The identification is never complete. If it were, the play would be merely a piece of flattery. But Miller has offered his audience an escape they do not deserve. He has allowed them a chance to think that John Proctor asserted the dignity of man against a benighted and outworn creed. Proctor did nothing of the kind. Proctor asserted the dignity of man against man. Man is the antagonist against which human dignity must always be defended; not against Puritanism, not against Nazism or communism, or McCarthyism, not against the Germans or the Russians or the Chinese, not against the Middle Ages or the Roman Empire. As long as we identify the evil in the world with some particular creed or with some other people remote in time or place, we flatter ourselves and cheapen the dignity and greatness of those who resist evil. The Germans, we say, or the Russians are inhuman beasts who trample humanity in the mud. We would never do such a thing. Belsen is in Germany. Salem Village is in the seventeenth century. It is a comforting and specious thought. It allows us to escape from the painful knowledge that has informed the great religions, knowledge incidentally that the Puritans always kept before them, the knowledge that all of us are capable of evil. The glory of human dignity is that any man may show it. The tragedy is that we are all equally capable of denying it.

—Edmund S. Morgan, "Arthur Miller's *The Crucible* and the Salem Witch Trials: A Historian's View," *The Golden and the Grazen World: Papers in Literature and History 1650–1800,* ed. John M. Wallace (Berkeley: University of California Press, 1985), pp. 185–86

❖

DENNIS WELLAND ON MILLER'S USE OF HISTORICAL
SOURCES IN *THE CRUCIBLE*

[Dennis Welland (b. 1919) is a professor of American
literature at Victoria University of Manchester in
Manchester, England. He is the author of *Wilfred
Owen: A Critical Study* (1960), *The Pre-Raphaelites in
Literature and Art* (1969), and several books on Arthur
Miller. In the following extract, Welland shows how
thoroughly Miller studied the historical sources for the
Salem witchcraft in writing *The Crucible* and how he
transformed that material into keen psychological por-
traits of the central figures.]

Miller provides a note on the historical accuracy of *The Crucible*
which indicates the care he has taken over it, and reference to
Marion Starkey's account or to the primary sources will quickly
substantiate this. (As many as possible of the original docu-
ments bearing on the events and the trials were collated in a
three-volume typescript in Essex County in 1938; that this was
a Works Progress Administration project provides yet another
instance of the influence—unexpected, belated, and indirect
this time—of the Depression on Miller's work.)

Reference to one primary source, for example, *A Modest
Inquiry into the Nature of Witchcraft,* written in 1697 by John
Hale will demonstrate an obvious identity between Miller's
character in *The Crucible* and the man who wrote at the time: 'I
observed in the prosecution of these affairs, that there was in
the Justices, Judges and others concerned, a conscientious
endeavour to do the thing that was right'. Nevertheless, he is
not easy in his own conscience, though what he questions is
legal procedure rather than witchcraft itself: 'We may hence
see ground to fear that there hath been a great deal of innocent
blood shed in the Christian World, by proceeding upon unsafe
principles, in condemning persons for Malefick Witchcraft'.
Hale is, however, still convinced that witchcraft may exist and
that vigilance must be maintained: 'Seeing we have been too
hard against supposed Malefick Witchcraft, let us take heed we
do not on the contrary, become too favourable to divining
Witchcraft [i.e. fortune telling]'.

The note of uncertainty, of suspended judgment, is very close to the keynote of *The Crucible,* which I find in the constant recurrence, on the lips of many different characters, of the phrase 'I think'. Much of the play could be summarised in Yeats's lines:

> The best lack all conviction, while the worst
> Are full of passionate intensity.

It is not so much a story of two ideologies in conflict as a story of conscientious endeavour in an uncertain world. This emerges with particular force and clarity in Act II, in, for example, such exchanges as this, in which Elizabeth Proctor tells her husband what she has heard from Mary Warren:

> ELIZABETH: The Deputy Governor promise hanging if they'll not confess, John. The town's gone wild, I think. She speak of Abigail, and I thought she were a saint, to hear her . . .
> PROCTOR: Oh, it is a black mischief.
> ELIZABETH: I think you must go to Salem, John. I think so. You must tell them it is a fraud.

Joe Keller had asked in vain for guidance: no one could give it to him. Willy Loman's bewilderment at Charley, who had never told his son what to do, is the bewilderment of the man who has confidently inculcated in his own sons a complete set of values that have turned out to be wrong (just as Ben's advice to Biff, 'Never fight fair with a stranger, boy', is, in its context, implicitly criticised). In *The Crucible* the wiser characters do not presume to dictate any one's duty to him, for that would be asking him to hand over his conscience. Moreover, they themselves are too perplexed by the conflicting implications of the issues to be dogmatic. Elizabeth's quietly-delivered suggestions here are the thoughts of a worried but honest mind spoken aloud for her husband's benefit, and he replies in the same key: 'I'll think on it . . . I think it is not easy to prove she's a fraud, and the town gone so silly'. Far from indicating a limited vocabulary, either of character or author, the repetition of this formula 'I think' is in fact a very skilfully-managed way of suggesting the scruples, the misgivings, and the conscientious earnestness which are all that these people can bring against the diabolic impetus of the witch-hunt. It is significant that

Miller chose to dramatise the story of John Proctor, the plain farmer, rather than the equally well-documented story of George Burrough, the minister, who was also accused of witchcraft and hanged for it. Miller's invention of Proctor's earlier adultery with Abigail is not the outcome of a mercenary desire to add a spice of sensationalism to the play. It is a similar insistence on the human vulnerability of a man who is not a saint, not even an ordained minister fortified by a theological training, but just a decent man trying to understand and to translate into action the dictates of his conscience, trying to do, not what he *feels*, but what he *thinks* is right.

—Dennis Welland, *Arthur Miller: The Playwright* (London: Methuen, 1979; 3rd ed. 1985), pp. 56–58

ROBERT A. MARTIN ON THE REVEREND JOHN HALE

[Robert A. Martin (b. 1930) is a professor of English at the University of Michigan. He is the editor of *The Theatre Essays of Arthur Miller* (1978) and *The Writer's Craft: Hopwood Lectures 1965–1981* (1982). In this extract, Martin asserts that the Reverend John Hale embodies the growing awareness of the illegality and immorality of the Salem witch trials.]

On a larger scale, Miller brings together the forces of personal and social malfunction through the arrival of the Reverend John Hale, who appears, appropriately, in the midst of a bitter quarrel among Proctor, Parris, and Thomas Putnam over deeds and land boundaries. Hale, in life as in the play, had encountered witchcraft previously and was called to Salem to determine if the Devil was in fact responsible for the illness of the afflicted children. In the play, he conceives of himself, Miller says, "much as a young doctor on his first call":

> [*He appears loaded down with half a dozen heavy books.*]
> HALE: Pray you, someone take these!

PARRIS [*delighted*]: Mr. Hale! Oh! it's good to see you again! [*Taking some books*] My, they're heavy!
HALE [*setting down his books*]: They must be; they are weighted with authority.

Hale's entrance at this particular point in the play is significant in that he interrupts an argument based on private and secular interests to bring "authority" to the question of witchcraft. His confidence in himself and his subsequent examination of the girls and Tituba (Parris's slave who inadvertently started the entire affair) represent and foreshadow the arrival of outside religious authority in the community. As an outsider who has come to weigh the evidence, Hale also helps to elevate the issue from a local to a regional level, and from an unofficial to an official theological inquiry. His heavy books of authority also symbolically anticipate the heavy authority of the judges who, as he will realize too late, are as susceptible to misinterpreting testimony based on spectral evidence as he is:

HALE [*with a tasty love of intellectual pursuit*]: Here is all the invisible world, caught, defined, and calculated. In these books the Devil stands stripped of all his brute disguises. Here are all your familiar spirits—your incubi and succubi; your witches that go by land, by air, and by sea; your wizards of the night and of the day. Have no fear now—we shall find him out if he has come among us, and I mean to crush him utterly if he has shown his face!

The Reverend Hale is an extremely interesting figure historically, and following the trials he set down an account of his repentance entitled *A Modest Inquiry into the Nature of Witchcraft* (Boston, 1702). Although he was at first as overly zealous in his pursuit of witches as everyone else, very much as Miller has portrayed him in *The Crucible,* Hale began to be tormented by doubts early in the proceedings. His uncertainty concerning the reliability of the witnesses and their testimony was considerably heightened when his own wife was also accused of being a witch. Hale appears to have been as tortured spiritually and as dedicated to the "middle way" in his later life as Miller has portrayed him in *The Crucible.* Five years after Salem, he wrote in his *Inquiry:*

The middle way is commonly the way of truth. And if any can shew me a better middle way than I have here laid down, I shall be ready to embrace it: But the conviction must not be by vinegar or drollery, but by strength of argument. . . . I have had a deep sence of the sad consequence of mistakes in matters Capital; and their impossibility of recovering when compleated. And what grief of heart it brings to a tender conscience, to have been unwittingly encouraging of the Sufferings of the innocent.

Hale further commented that although he presently believed the executions to be the unfortunate result of human error, the integrity of the court officials was unquestionable: "I observed in the prosecution of these affairs, that there was in the Justices, Judges and others concerned, a conscientious endeavour to do the thing that was right. And to that end they consulted the Presidents [Precedents] of former times and precepts laid down by Learned Writers about Witchcraft."

In *The Crucible,* Hale's examination of Tituba is very nearly an edited transcription of her testimony at the trial of Sarah Good, who is the first person Abigail accuses of consorting with the Devil. At the time of the trials, Sarah Good had long been an outcast member of the Salem community, "unpopular because of her slothfulness, her sullen temper, and her poverty; she had recently taken to begging, an occupation the Puritans detested." When she was about to be hanged, her minister, the Reverend Nicholas Noyes, made a last appeal to her for a confession and said he knew she was a witch. Her prophetic reply was probably seen later as proof of her guilt when she said to Noyes: "you are a lyer; I am no more a Witch than you are a Wizard, and if you take away my Life, God will give you Blood to drink." A few years after she was hanged, Reverend Noyes died as a result of a sudden and severe hemorrhage.

Largely through the Reverend Hale, Miller reflects the change that took place in Salem from an initial belief in the justice of the court to a suspicion that testimony based on spectral evidence was insufficient for execution. This transformation begins to reveal itself in Act Two, as Hale tells Francis Nurse that the court will clear his wife of the charges against her: "Believe me, Mr. Nurse, if Rebecca Nurse be tainted, then nothing's left to stop the whole green world from burning. Let you rest upon the justice of the court; the court will send her home, I know it." By Act Three, however, Hale's confidence in the justice of the court has been badly shaken by the arrest and conviction of people like Rebecca Nurse who were highly respected members of the church and community. Hale, like his historical model, has discovered that "the whole green world" is burning indeed, and fears that he has helped to set the fire.

—Robert A. Martin, "Arthur Miller's *The Crucible:* Background and Sources," *Essays on Modern American Drama: Williams, Miller, Albee and Shepard,* ed. Dorothy Parker (Toronto: University of Toronto Press, 1987), pp. 85–87

Iska Alter on the Role of Women in *The Crucible*

[Iska Alter is a professor of English at Hofstra University and author of *The Good Man's Dilemma: Social Criticism in the Fiction of Bernard Malamud* (1981). In this extract, Alter studies the role of women in Miller's play and maintains that it presents two versions of female power, one represented by the accusers and the other by positive figures such as Rebecca Nurse and Elizabeth Proctor.]

The design of *The Crucible* attempts to make visible two discrete, self-contained and antagonistic expressions of female power to test their legitimacy as authentic definitions of sexual desire. The externalized contest between the impulse that betrays, embodied in the group of accusers led by Abigail Williams, and the force that nurtures, personified by the figures of Rebecca Nurse and Elizabeth Proctor, shapes the choices made by John Proctor on his road to martyrdom. This schematic moral division is clearly drawn. The young women compelled by the anarchic strength of the erotic destroy the righteous and the dutiful for whom instinct is disciplined or submerged in service to family and community. But as the play unfolds, its melodramatic absolutism collapses under the pressure of Puritan authority suspicious of both views, because any knowledge of desire is potentially a transgression; and the too easily assumed virtue that seemed to inform John Proctor's decisions grows darker, more complex and more difficult.

There is no question that the girls—Betty Parris, Ruth Putnam, Mercy Lewis, Mary Warren, and, most especially, Abigail Williams—are suspect and possibly dangerous. Their sexually charged presence in the forest, the Puritan landscape of nightmare, is an explicit violation of publicly affirmed communal norms as well as private standards of right conduct insisted upon by a male-authorized social order sustained by a patriarchal, woman-fearing theology ⟨. . .⟩

Having named desire as unnatural, this repressive culture has condemned an inherent, normal biological process as aberrant, criminal, or, worse yet, as profoundly evil, the essential principle of demonic command. The journey into the woods, undertaken as an attempt to deal with and manage the consequences of inchoate sexuality, renders these young women outlaws. Within the dramatic action of the play, the sexually fallen Abigail particularly represents the release of this insurgent, destabilizing horrific energy ⟨. . .⟩

By challenging the apparently decent men and women of Salem, the young women, led by the knowing Abigail, act to scourge hypocrisy, punish its practitioners, and exact revenge for their socially determined impotence. Rebecca Nurse, for example, is attacked because she seems able to control and direct nature's fecundity ("You think it God's work you should never lose a child, nor grandchild either"); and Elizabeth Proctor because her righteousness seems an instrument for the denial of her fundamental sensuality. For both women, the condemnation demands a necessary reevaluation of the assumptions that conditioned their lives. Rebecca, who has never known suffering, accepts her pain, therefore granting that she cannot master the ambiguous force of natural energy and welcoming her martyrdom. Elizabeth Proctor confesses her complicity in her husband's downfall. ("I have read my heart this three month, John. . . . I have sins of my own to count. It needs a cold wife to prompt lechery.") She finds blessing in acknowledging her participation in a series of complex betrayals provoked by erotic uncertainty, and, with curious irony, Elizabeth is permitted to survive her adulterous if heroic husband because of a pregnancy that in the most obvious fashion reaffirms the sexuality she initially has chosen to repudiate.

—Iska Alter, "Betrayal and Blessedness: Explorations of Feminine Power in *The Crucible, A View from the Bridge,* and *After the Fall," Feminist Rereadings of Modern American Drama,* ed. June Schlueter (Rutherford, NJ: Fairleigh Dickinson University Press, 1989), pp. 120–21, 123

RICHARD G. SACHARINE ON SOCIETY AND OPPRESSION IN *THE CRUCIBLE*

[Richard G. Sacharine (b. 1938) teaches in the theatre department at the University of Utah. He is the author of *The Plays of Edward Bond* (1976) and *From Class to Caste in American Drama* (1991), from which the following extract is taken. Here, Sacharine begins by noting that both the Salem witch trials and the communist "witch hunts" of the 1950s erupted in secure and prosperous societies. He then goes on to examine specific trials in *The Crucible* and their effects on the principal characters.]

One of the ironies of the Salem tragedy and the Cold War is that both arose in times of relative prosperity following a period when the people's survival was very much in doubt. World War II (and the Depression preceding it) had ended for the United States, while the battle of the Puritan settlers with nature and the Indians was just beginning to yield results. In both cases, consequently, the extraordinary discipline and sense of purpose which had seen them through the crisis was weakening. Freed of the necessity for absolute unity, some people began to question aspects of public policy and demand new freedoms. Salem was a theocracy—a system of government incorporating the principles of a state church and presumably acting as the temporal arm of God. It is a system under which dissidence cannot exist, for to be in opposition to religious leadership is punishable by civil law, and disagreement with the government becomes heresy.

The strength of a messianic state is that it commands unity on all levels. Its weakness is that it assigns all evil to its opposition, and necessarily associates that opposition with the evil one, the Devil. Judge Danforth phrases it best in *The Crucible:* "You must understand, sir, that a person is either with this court or he must be counted against it, there is no road in between."

The problem is that an individual may oppose a church or a government for reasons other than witchcraft or communism. John Proctor stays away from church because he finds the Reverend Mr. Parris to be materialistic, but this does not make him an atheist. Though a person might understandably hide his practice of witchcraft, it does not necessarily follow that *everything* hidden is witchcraft—as the prosecution of Martha Corey on the evidence that she refused to show her husband the books she read indicates. One may also feel guilty for sins of less than apocalyptic import. John Proctor's inability to remember the Seventh Commandment is not diabolically inspired revulsion to Scripture, but rather shame over his adultery with Abigail Williams.

The Reverend John Hale is a sincere scholar of witchcraft, but experts tend to define problems in terms of their expertise, relevant or not. In the service of the court, a bureaucrat like Ezekiel Cheever will find what he is told to find without troubling his conscience over its consequences. Furthermore, though war against the Devil is holy, not all those who make accusations are. Some are to be pitied, like Ann Putnam, who, driven half mad by the infant deaths of seven of her eight children, alleviates her guilt by accusing Rebecca Nurse, who has had eleven healthy children. Some are to be condemned. Ann's husband, Thomas, sees the trials as a means of gaining the land of his convicted neighbors, and Abigail Williams's longing for John Proctor provides the motive for her condemnation of Elizabeth Proctor.

Two factors complicate the accusation and courtroom procedure: the presence of self-induced and mass hysteria, and the permitting of spectral evidence. In Act II, Scene 2, of *The*

Crucible, we are shown an Abigail who has come to believe her own accusations. She is like a consummate actress who has made herself the role she plays, and who can extend her aura to her fellow perfomers and to the audience. Mary Warren, the Proctors' impressionable servant and one of the accusing girls, describes the sensation which overcomes her in court: "I feel a clamp around my neck and I cannot breathe air; and then—I hear a voice, a screamin' voice, and it were my voice—and all · at once I remembered everything she done to me!"

Later, when Mary tries to confess to the judges that the accusers were pretending, Abigail and the girls turn the same hypnotic hysteria on her that they used on courtroom observers. In a chilling scene, the girls conjure up a diabolic force which their imaginations make so palpable that Mary is reduced to a screaming acquiescence to their accusations, leading to the arrest of John Proctor.

Spectral evidence was the claim by a witness or a victim—unverifiable even by others who were present—that the witch's spirit had engaged in acts of torture. The discomfort of the victim was the proof of the crime, and the clairvoyance of the witness identified the criminal. That there was no evidence defined the crime as witchcraft, a thought crime. "Witchcraft is *ipso facto,* on its face and by its nature, an invisible crime, is it not? Therefore, who may possibly be witness to it? The witch and the victim. None other. Now we cannot hope that the witch will accuse herself, granted? Therefore, we must rely upon her victims—and they do testify, the children certainly do testify." Thus, in cases of suspected witchcraft, punishment could legitimately follow an accusation of the contemplation of (conspiracy to commit) crime—a condition blurring the distinction between civil crime and religious sin.

As was pointed out earlier, Salem was unique among witchcraft trials in that no confessor was executed. Since defense was virtually impossible, after the first hangings only the strongest willed of the defendants maintained their innocence. The Reverend John Hale, initially an official of the court, loses faith in the justice of its decision and finds himself counseling those he believes innocent to confess, solely for the purpose of saving their lives. In *Darkness at Noon,* Ivanoff, who knows

Rubashov is not guilty, and Gletkin, his enemy, differ only in the *way* they expect to induce Rubashov to confess. As Lampell noted, confession was the only way off the blacklist. When the New York City Commission voted in 1955 not to allow Arthur Miller to make a film about teenage gangs and the urban problem, one of the commissioners said: "I'm not calling him a Communist. My objection is that he refuses to repent."

John Proctor eventually confesses to a compact with the Devil in order to save his life, only to recant when faced with the confession's second requirement—the naming of others in the compact. Such a naming was necessary not only as an act of contrition, it was necessary also to prove that there was a compact at all. In crimes of thought, there is no evidence except the witnesses' testimony concerning the defendant's spirit, whatever its manifestation. Once we assume a conspiracy exists, then those who testify to bad character are seen as repentant, while those who testify to good character are seen as potential conspirators themselves. For example, in *The Crucible* those Salem citizens who signed a petition affirming the good character of Martha Corey, Rebecca Nurse, and Elizabeth Proctor are "arrested for examination."

> —Richard G. Sacharine, *From Class to Caste in American Drama: Political and Social Themes Since the 1930s* (Westport, CT: Greenwood Press, 1991), pp. 84–86

JAMES J. MARTINE ON THE METAPHORICAL USE OF THE CRUCIBLE

[James J. Martine (b. 1937) is the head of the Graduate Program in English at St. Bonaventure University. He has written *American Novelists 1910–1945* (1981) and edited essays on Arthur Miller (1979) and Eugene O'Neill (1993). In this extract from his study of *The Crucible,* Martine examines the metaphorical use of the crucible (a test or trial) and its significance to the play and to American society at large.]

A crucible is a severe test or a hard trial. More pointedly, the term also refers to a container that can resist great heat and is used for melting and calcining ores; most commonly the end product that comes out of the crucible is a purer high-grade steel. As Danforth quite directly warns Proctor, "it is my duty to tell you this. We burn a hot fire here; it melts down all conceal-ment."

The title obviously, then, refers to the test or hard trial that Proctor undergoes. With all concealment melted down, the product—Proctor's moral constitution—is of a higher quality. On the other hand, we must not overlook the significance of the fact that, as Miller well knew, a crucible is a melting pot—what this nation claims itself to be. Thus, *The Crucible* may be said to stand as a figure for America itself. As such, Miller's play is an examination of America, from its seventeenth-century beginnings to the events of the 1950s. Miller's ambiv-alent evaluation of the continuity from the Puritans to the present comes to the conclusion that "they believed, in short, that they held in their steady hands the candle that would light the world. We have inherited this belief, and it has helped and hurt us." ⟨. . .⟩

While the play was at first seen as an allegory about the McCarthy witch-hunt, its real importance could be appreciated only after the initial furor died down. *The Crucible is* about witchcraft at Salem in 1692, and it *was* inspired by the social and political climate in the United States in the 1950s—Miller is the first to admit that—but these specific historical events do not account for the play's continuing popularity throughout the world. At the 1965 National Theatre production of the play in London, for example, Miller overheard a young woman whis-per to her escort, "Didn't this have something to do with that American Senator—what was his name?" Miller concedes "that it felt marvellous that McCarthy was what's-his-name while *The Crucible* was *The Crucible* still." Moreover, and perhaps even more to the point, the playwright recalls being greatly affected in 1988 upon meeting Nien Cheng, the 70-year-old author of an account of her six-year imprisonment during China's Cultural Revolution, who, with tears in her eyes, related the play, which she had seen in a Shanghai theater, to her own experience.

Many people abroad have little or no clue as to who McCarthy was or what McCarthyism was about. One of the resources upon which the play draws, clear to someone with Nien Cheng's experience, may be Miller's contention that "the very idea of authority was fraudulent."

Without a broader message, *The Crucible* might have perished in the 1950s or become a historical oddity of interest only to historians of New England and people curious about witchcraft. Since the play transcends both aspects of its historicity, its endurance and effectiveness must be found in other, grander matters. It may be that beyond Salem and beyond the witch-hunts of the 1950s, Miller had touched truths of the human spirit. The play continues to be produced because it addresses matters that are of continuing concern to intelligent men and women. The play possesses themes and underlying universals which apparently transcend time and place, including national borders. It is produced in China, the Soviet Union, continental Europe, and Latin America in addition to England and the United States.

Miller's own estimate suggests that the sun barely sets on this play. Scarcely a week goes by when it is not produced somewhere in the world. By Miller's kenning, the importance of this play will not be measured by the number of performances, financial rewards, or theatrical and literary affinities to earlier or later works, but by its influence upon people, young and old, and such impetus as it lends to inspiring "their minds in relation to liberty, in relation to the rights of people."

—James J. Martine, The Crucible: *Politics, Property and Pretense* (New York: Twayne, 1993), pp. 13–15

Works by Arthur Miller

Situation Normal. 1944.

Focus. 1945.

All My Sons. 1947.

Death of a Salesman: Certain Private Conversations in Two Acts and a Requiem. 1949.

An Enemy of the People by Henrik Ibsen (adaptor). 1951.

The Crucible. 1953.

A View from the Bridge with *A Memory of Two Mondays⟩: Two One-Act Plays.* 1955.

Collected Plays. 1957–81. 2 vols.

The Misfits. 1961.

Jane's Blanket. 1963.

After the Fall. 1964.

Incident at Vichy. 1965.

I Don't Need You Any More: Stories. 1967, 1987 (as *The Misfits and Other Stories*).

The Price. 1968.

In Russia (with Inge Morath). 1969.

The Portable Arthur Miller. Ed. Harold Clurman. 1971.

The Creation of the World and Other Business. 1973.

In the Country (with Inge Morath). 1977.

Theatre Essays. Ed. Robert A. Martin. 1978.

Chinese Encounters (with Inge Morath). 1979.

Eight Plays. 1981.

Playing for Time: A Screenplay. 1981.

The American Clock. 1982.

Elegy for a Lady. 1982.

Some Kind of Love Story. 1983.

Salesman in Beijing. 1984.

The Archbishop's Ceiling. 1984.

Two-Way Mirror: A Double-Bill of Elegy for a Lady and Some Kind of Love Story. 1984.

Playing for Time: A Full-Length Stage Play. 1985.

Danger: Memory! A Double-Bill of I Can't Remember Anything and Clara. 1986.

Timebends: A Life. 1987.

Conversations with Arthur Miller. Ed. Matthew C. Roudane. 1987.

Plays: One. 1988.

The Archbishop's Ceiling; The American Clock. 1988.

Plays: Two. 1988.

The Golden Years and The Man Who Had All the Luck. 1989.

Early Plays. 1989.

On Censorship and Laughter. 1990.

Plays: Three. 1990.

Everybody Wins: A Screenplay. 1990.

The Last Yankee. 1991.

The Ride Down Mount Morgan. 1991.

Homely Girl: A Life (with Louise Bourgeois). 1992. 2 vols.

Broken Glass. 1994.

The Last Yankee; with a New Essay, About Theatre Language; and Broken Glass. 1994.

Plays: Four. 1994.

Works about
Arthur Miller and
The Crucible

Adam, Julie. *Versions of Heroism in Modern American Drama: Redefinitions by Miller, Williams, O'Neill, and Anderson.* New York: St. Martin's Press, 1991.

Bergeron, David M. "Arthur Miller's *The Crucible* and Nathaniel Hawthorne: Some Parallels." *English Journal* 58 (1969): 47–55.

Bhatia, Santosh K. *Arthur Miller: Social Drama as Tragedy.* New Delhi: Arnold-Heinemann, 1985.

Bigsby, C. W. E. *Confrontation and Commitment: A Study of Contemporary American Drama.* Columbia: University of Missouri Press, 1967.

————, ed. *File on Miller.* London: Methuen, 1988.

Bloom, Harold, ed. *Arthur Miller.* New York: Chelsea House, 1987.

Blumberg, Paul. "Sociology and Social Literature: Work Alienation in the Plays of Arthur Miller." *American Quarterly* 21 (1969): 291–310.

Bonnet, Jean-Marie. "Society vs. the Individual in Arthur Miller's *The Crucible.*" *English Studies* 63 (1982): 32–36.

Broussard, Louis. *American Drama: Contemporary Allegory from Eugene O'Neill to Tennessee Williams.* Norman: University of Oklahoma Press, 1962.

Calarco, N. Joseph. "Production as Criticism: Miller's *The Crucible.*" *Educational Theatre Journal* 29 (1977): 354–61.

Cohn, Ruby. *Dialogue in American Drama.* Bloomington: Indiana University Press, 1971.

Corrigan, Robert W., ed. *Arthur Miller: A Collection of Critical Essays.* Englewood Cliffs, NJ: Prentice-Hall, 1969.

DelFattore, Joan. "Fueling the Fire of Hell: A Reply to the Censors of *The Crucible.*" In *Censored Books: Critical Viewpoints,* ed. Nicholas J. Karolides and Lee Burress. Metuchen, NJ: Scarecrow Press, 1993, pp. 201–8.

Ditsky, John. "Stone, Fire and Light: Approaches to *The Crucible.*" *North Dakota Quarterly* 46, No. 2 (1978): 65–72.

Douglass, James W. "Miller's *The Crucible:* Which Witch Is Which?" *Renascence* 15 (1963): 145–51.

Driver, Tom F. "Strength and Weakness in Arthur Miller." *Tulane Drama Review* 4, No. 4 (May 1960): 45–52.

Dukore, Bernard F. Death of a Salesman *and* The Crucible. Atlantic Highlands, NJ: Humanities Press, 1989.

Evans, Richard I. *Psychology and Arthur Miller.* New York: Dutton, 1969.

Ferres, John H. "Still in the Present Tense: *The Crucible* Today." *University College Quarterly* 17 (1972): 8–18.

Foulkes, A. P. *Literature and Propaganda.* London: Methuen, 1983.

Ganz, Arthur. "The Silence of Arthur Miller." *Drama Survey* 3 (1963): 224–37.

Gassner, John. *Form and Idea in Modern Theatre.* New York: Dryden, 1956.

Greenfield, Thomas Allen. *Work and the Work Ethic in American Drama 1920–1970.* Columbia: University of Missouri Press, 1982.

Hayman, Ronald. *Arthur Miller.* London: William Heinemann, 1970.

Heilman, Robert B. *The Iceman, the Arsonist and the Troubled Agent: Tragedy and Melodrama on the Modern Stage.* Seattle: University of Washington Press, 1973.

Liston, William T. "John Proctor's Playing in *The Crucible.*" *Midwest Quarterly* 20 (1979): 394–403.

McCollom, William G. *Tragedy.* New York: Macmillan, 1957.

McGill, William J., Jr. "The Crucible of History: Arthur Miller's John Proctor." *New England History* 54 (1981): 258–64.

Martin, Robert A., ed. *Arthur Miller: New Perspectives.* Englewood Cliffs, NJ: Prentice-Hall, 1982.

Martine, James J., ed. *Critical Essays on Arthur Miller.* Boston: G. K. Hall, 1979.

Miller, Jeanne-Marie A. "Odets, Miller, and Communism." *CLA Journal* 19 (1976): 484–93.

Mottram, Eric. "Arthur Miller: The Development of a Political Dramatist in America." In *American Theatre* (Stratford-upon-Avon Studies 10), ed. John Russell Brown and Bernard Harris. London: Edward Arnold, 1967, pp. 127–62.

O'Neal, Michael J. "History, Myth, and Name Magic in Arthur Miller's *The Crucible.*" *CLIO* 12 (1983): 111–22.

Panikkar, N. Bhaskara. *Individual Morality and Social Happiness in Arthur Miller.* Atlantic Highlands, NJ: Humanities Press, 1982.

Pearson, Michelle. "John Proctor and the Crucible of Individuation in Arthur Miller's *The Crucible.*" *Studies in American Drama 1945–Present* 6 (1991): 15–27.

Popkin, Henry. "Arthur Miller's *The Crucible.*" *College English* 26 (1964–65): 139–46.

Prudhoe, John. "Arthur Miller and the Tradition of Tragedy." *English Studies* 43 (1962): 430–39.

Scanlan, Tom. *Family, Drama, and American Dreams.* Westport, CT: Greenwood Press, 1978.

Schlueter, June, and James K. Flanagan. *Arthur Miller.* New York: Ungar, 1987.

Schroeder, Patricia R. *The Presence of the Past in Modern American Drama.* Rutherford, NJ: Fairleigh Dickinson University Press, 1989.

Spindler, Michael. *American Literature and Social Change: William Dean Howells to Arthur Miller.* Bloomington: Indiana University Press, 1983.

Tien, Morris Wei-hsin. "The 'Witchcraft Delusion' in Three American Plays." *American Studies* 18 (1988): 29–58.

Trowbridge, Clinton W. "Arthur Miller: Between Pathos and Tragedy." *Modern Drama* 10 (1967): 221–32.

Vogel, Dan. *The Three Masks of American Tragedy.* Baton Rouge: Louisiana State University Press, 1974.

Williams, Raymond. *Modern Tragedy.* Stanford: Stanford University Press, 1966.

Index of
Themes and Ideas